PRIVACY AND IDENTITY PROTECTION

GOVERNMENT REPORTS ON INFORMATION SECURITY AND TECHNOLOGY FOR MARCH 2019

PRIVACY AND IDENTITY PROTECTION

Additional books and e-books in this series can be found
on Nova's website under the Series tab.

PRIVACY AND IDENTITY PROTECTION

GOVERNMENT REPORTS ON INFORMATION SECURITY AND TECHNOLOGY FOR MARCH 2019

MATHIAS SCHWEITZER
EDITOR

Copyright © 2019 by Nova Science Publishers, Inc.

All rights reserved. No part of this book may be reproduced, stored in a retrieval system or transmitted in any form or by any means: electronic, electrostatic, magnetic, tape, mechanical photocopying, recording or otherwise without the written permission of the Publisher.

We have partnered with Copyright Clearance Center to make it easy for you to obtain permissions to reuse content from this publication. Simply navigate to this publication's page on Nova's website and locate the "Get Permission" button below the title description. This button is linked directly to the title's permission page on copyright.com. Alternatively, you can visit copyright.com and search by title, ISBN, or ISSN.

For further questions about using the service on copyright.com, please contact:
Copyright Clearance Center
Phone: +1-(978) 750-8400   Fax: +1-(978) 750-4470   E-mail: info@copyright.com.

NOTICE TO THE READER

The Publisher has taken reasonable care in the preparation of this book, but makes no expressed or implied warranty of any kind and assumes no responsibility for any errors or omissions. No liability is assumed for incidental or consequential damages in connection with or arising out of information contained in this book. The Publisher shall not be liable for any special, consequential, or exemplary damages resulting, in whole or in part, from the readers' use of, or reliance upon, this material. Any parts of this book based on government reports are so indicated and copyright is claimed for those parts to the extent applicable to compilations of such works.

Independent verification should be sought for any data, advice or recommendations contained in this book. In addition, no responsibility is assumed by the Publisher for any injury and/or damage to persons or property arising from any methods, products, instructions, ideas or otherwise contained in this publication.

This publication is designed to provide accurate and authoritative information with regard to the subject matter covered herein. It is sold with the clear understanding that the Publisher is not engaged in rendering legal or any other professional services. If legal or any other expert assistance is required, the services of a competent person should be sought. FROM A DECLARATION OF PARTICIPANTS JOINTLY ADOPTED BY A COMMITTEE OF THE AMERICAN BAR ASSOCIATION AND A COMMITTEE OF PUBLISHERS.

Additional color graphics may be available in the e-book version of this book.

Library of Congress Cataloging-in-Publication Data

ISBN: 978-1-53615-848-9

Published by Nova Science Publishers, Inc. † New York

CONTENTS

Preface		**vii**
Chapter 1	Data Breaches: Range of Consumer Risks Highlights Limitations of Identity Theft Services *United States Government Accountability Office*	**1**
Chapter 2	Internet Privacy and Data Security: Additional Federal Authority Could Enhance Consumer Protection and Provide Flexibility *Alicia Puente Cackley*	**45**
Chapter 3	DOD Space Acquisitions: Including Users Early and Often in Software Development Could Benefit Programs *United States Government Accountability Office*	**57**
Index		**119**
Related Nova Publications		**123**

PREFACE

This book is a comprehensive compilation of all reports, testimony, correspondence and other publications issued by the GAO (Government Accountability Office) during the month of March, grouped according to the topics: Information Security and Technology.

Chapter 1 - Recent large-scale data breaches of public and private entities have put hundreds of millions of people at risk of identity theft or other harm. GAO was asked to review issues related to consumers' options to address risks of harm from data breaches. This report, among other things, examines information and expert views on the effectiveness of consumer options to address data breach risks. GAO analyzed available data on options, collected and analyzed related documentation, conducted a literature review of studies, and interviewed a nongeneralizable sample of 35 experts (from academia, government entities, consumer and industry organizations) and identity theft service providers to reflect a range of views.

Chapter 2 - This is an edited, reformatted and augmented accessible version of the United States Government Accountability Office Testimony Before the Permanent Subcommittee on Investigations, Committee on Homeland Security and Governmental Affairs, U.S. Senate, Publication No. GAO-19-427T, dated March 7, 2019.

Chapter 3 - Over the next 5 years, DOD plans to spend over $65 billion on its space system acquisitions portfolio, including many systems that rely on software for key capabilities. However, software-intensive space systems have had a history of significant schedule delays and billions of dollars in cost growth. Senate and House reports accompanying the National Defense Authorization Act for Fiscal Year 2017 contained provisions for GAO to review challenges in software-intensive DOD space programs. This report addresses, among other things, (1) the extent to which these programs have involved users; and (2) what software-specific management challenges, if any, programs faced. To do this work, GAO reviewed four major space defense programs with cost growth or schedule delays caused, in part, by software. GAO reviewed applicable statutes and DOD policies and guidance that identified four characteristics of effective user engagement. GAO reviewed program documentation; and interviewed program officials, contractors, and space systems users. GAO also analyzed program metrics, test and evaluation reports, and external program assessments.

In: Government Reports …
Editor: Mathias Schweitzer

ISBN: 978-1-53615-848-9
© 2019 Nova Science Publishers, Inc.

Chapter 1

DATA BREACHES: RANGE OF CONSUMER RISKS HIGHLIGHTS LIMITATIONS OF IDENTITY THEFT SERVICES[*]

United States Government Accountability Office

ABBREVIATIONS

CFPB	Consumer Financial Protection Bureau
FTC	Federal Trade Commission
IRS	Internal Revenue Service
OMB	Office of Management and Budget
OPM	Office of Personnel Management
PIN	personal identification number

---

[*] This is an edited, reformatted and augmented version of the United States Government Accountability Office Report to Congressional Requesters, Publication No. GAO-19-230, dated March 2019.

WHY GAO DID THIS STUDY

Recent large-scale data breaches of public and private entities have put hundreds of millions of people at risk of identity theft or other harm. GAO was asked to review issues related to consumers' options to address risks of harm from data breaches. This report, among other things, examines information and expert views on the effectiveness of consumer options to address data breach risks. GAO analyzed available data on options, collected and analyzed related documentation, conducted a literature review of studies, and interviewed a nongeneralizable sample of 35 experts (from academia, government entities, consumer and industry organizations) and identity theft service providers to reflect a range of views.

WHAT GAO RECOMMENDS

GAO reiterates a matter for congressional consideration and a recommendation from its 2017 report on identity theft services (GAO-17-254). In that report, GAO found that legislation requiring federal agencies that experience data breaches, including OPM, to offer certain levels of identity theft insurance coverage to affected individuals requires coverage levels that are likely unnecessary. Therefore, Congress should consider permitting agencies to determine the appropriate coverage level for such insurance. GAO also recommended the Office of Management and Budget (OMB) update its guidance for agency responses to data breaches, after analyzing the effectiveness of identity theft services relative to lower-cost alternatives. OMB did not agree or disagree and had not taken action as of early March 2019.

Data Breaches 3

WHAT GAO FOUND

No one solution can address the range of potential risks from a data breach, according to interviews with academic, consumer, government, and industry experts and documentation GAO reviewed. Perpetrators of fraud can use stolen personal information—such as account numbers, passwords, or Social Security numbers—to take out loans or seek medical care under someone else's name, or make unauthorized purchases on credit cards, among other crimes. Foreign state-based actors can use personal information to support espionage or other nefarious uses.

Public and private entities that experience a breach sometimes provide complimentary commercial identity theft services to affected individuals to help monitor their credit accounts or restore their identities in cases of identity theft, among other features. Consumers also may purchase the services. As of November 30, 2018, the Office of Personnel Management (OPM) had obligated about $421 million for a suite of credit and identity monitoring, insurance, and identity restoration services to offer to the approximately 22 million individuals affected by its 2015 data breaches. As of September 30, 2018, about 3 million had used the services and approximately 61 individuals had received payouts from insurance claims, for an average of $1,800 per claim. OPM re-competed and awarded a contract to the previously contracted company in December 2018.

GAO's review did not identify any studies that analyzed whether consumers who sign up for or purchase identity theft services were less subject to identity theft or detected financial or other fraud more or less quickly than those who monitored their own accounts for free. A few experts said consumers could sign up for such services if offered for free. Credit monitoring may be convenient for consumers and personalized restoration services may help identity theft victims recover their identities, but such services do not prevent fraud from happening in the first place. The services also do not prevent or directly address risks of nonfinancial harm such as medical identity theft.

Consumer, government, and industry experts highlighted other free options, including a credit freeze, which prevents one type of fraud. A

4 *United States Government Accountability Office*

freeze restricts businesses from accessing a person's credit report—and can prevent the illicit opening of a new account or loan in the person's name. A provision of federal law that took effect in September 2018 made it free for consumers to place or lift credit freezes quickly at the three nationwide consumer reporting agencies (Equifax, Experian, and TransUnion). Consumers also can regularly monitor their accounts and review their credit reports for free every 12 months. In addition, they can take advantage of free federal assistance such as the guidance on the Federal Trade Commission's IdentityTheft.gov website.

Finally, large amounts of personal information are outside of consumers' control and bad actors can use stolen information for years after a breach. Therefore, experts noted that data security at entities that hold such information—and efforts to make stolen information less useful for identity thieves, through use of new identity verification technologies, for example—are important ways to mitigate risks of harm for consumers.

March 27, 2019

The Honorable Frank Pallone
Chairman
Committee on Energy and Commerce
House of Representatives

The Honorable Jan Schakowsky
Chair
Subcommittee on Consumer Protection and Commerce
Committee on Energy and Commerce
House of Representatives

The Honorable Diana DeGette
Chair
Subcommittee on Oversight and Investigations
Committee on Energy and Commerce
House of Representatives

Data Breaches

Sensitive personal information—such as Social Security numbers or dates of birth—can be exposed in several ways, including on a very large scale through a data breach.[1] For example, major retail and hotel chains have suffered data breaches that exposed the identifying information, including financial account or Social Security numbers, of millions of people. Consumers whose information is exposed can be at risk of a range of harms, including identity theft or fraud. Consumers can try to prevent or mitigate these harms in a number of ways, such as monitoring their credit reports and credit card statements for suspicious activity, or placing a credit freeze that restricts access to their credit report. They also may enroll in free or fee-based identity theft services.[2] Private-sector and government entities that experienced data breaches have provided these services to millions of affected consumers.

In March 2017, we reported on the potential benefits and limitations of commercially available identity theft services and factors that affect public- and private-sector decision-making about them.[3] Since that time, additional large-scale data breaches have occurred and Congress passed legislation that enhances some of the options available to consumers to prevent or mitigate identity theft. You asked us to review issues related to actions consumers can take to address risks of harm from data breaches. This report examines (1) information and expert views on the effectiveness of options consumers can use to prevent or address the risks resulting from data breaches; and (2) federal assistance available to help consumers understand these options, including the status of one matter for congressional consideration and one recommendation relating to these issues in our 2017 report.

---

[1] A data breach generally refers to an unauthorized or unintentional exposure, disclosure, or loss of an organization's sensitive information. This information can include personally identifiable information, such as Social Security numbers, or financial information, such as credit card numbers. A data breach can be inadvertent, such as from the loss of an electronic device, or deliberate, such as from the theft of a device or a cyber-based attack by a malicious individual or group, agency insiders, foreign nations, or terrorists.

[2] We use "identity theft services" to refer to commercial products that generally provide tools intended to help consumers detect identity theft and restore their identity if it has been compromised.

[3] GAO, *Identity Theft Services: Services Offer Some Benefits but Are Limited in Preventing Fraud*, GAO-17-254 (Washington, D.C.: Mar. 30, 2017).

6 *United States Government Accountability Office*

To address the first objective, we conducted a literature review to identify any studies or independent research on the effectiveness of consumers' options for mitigating or preventing harm from exposure of personal information. We also searched for studies that examined consumer attitudes and behavior following data breaches, and harms to individuals from data breaches. We interviewed a nongeneralizable sample of experts and private companies that provide identity theft services to consumers.[4] Specifically, we interviewed representatives of 35 entities in the following categories: academic or independent research institution (4); consumer or privacy research and advocacy (10); industry association or identity theft service provider, or industry consultant (12); and federal or state government (9). We selected the experts and identity theft service providers to represent a range of perspectives. We also reviewed provisions in the Economic Growth, Regulatory Relief, and Consumer Protection Act, enacted in May 2018, that address credit freezes and fraud alerts (two tools for preventing one type of identity theft).[5] Furthermore, we reviewed the evidence collected for the 2017 GAO report on identity theft services.[6]

To address the second objective, we reviewed documentation and interviewed staff from the Federal Trade Commission (FTC), Consumer Financial Protection Bureau (CFPB), and Office of Personnel Management (OPM). We analyzed data from the company that contracted to provide identity theft services to individuals affected by two data breaches at OPM in 2015. We assessed the reliability of the data by interviewing agency officials and reviewing documentation about the systems used to store the data. We found the data to be reliable for

---

[4] Throughout this report, we use certain qualifiers when describing responses from interview participants, such as "few," "some," and "most." While we define few as a small number such as two or three, the specific quantification of other categories depends on the overall numbers of interviewees who addressed a specific topic, and is discussed in more detail in appendix I. We defined experts as those with academic research backgrounds or professional expertise gained from employment in consumer and industry policy organizations, as well as federal and state government staff with specific positions of responsibility in consumer protection.

[5] Pub. L. No. 115-174, § 301(a), 132 Stat. 1296, 1326 (2018) (codified at 15 U.S.C. § 1681c–1(i)).

[6] GAO-17-254.

Data Breaches 7

purposes of this reporting objective. We also reviewed documentation and interviewed agency staff about the development, implementation, and assessment of their consumer education materials and other resources and assistance. We compared these activities against a 2014 Executive Order on the security of consumer financial transactions, key practices for consumer education planning identified in our prior work, and federal standards for internal control.[7] In addition, we followed up on recommendations made in our 2017 report. For more information on our scope and methodology, including the organization representatives we interviewed, see appendix I.

We conducted this performance audit from November 2017 to March 2019 in accordance with generally accepted government auditing standards. Those standards require that we plan and perform the audit to obtain sufficient, appropriate evidence to provide a reasonable basis for our findings and conclusions based on our audit objectives. We believe that the evidence obtained provides a reasonable basis for our findings and conclusions based on our audit objectives.

BACKGROUND

Harm from Exposure of Personal Information

Individuals' sensitive personal information can be lost, stolen, or given away.[8] Once exposed, individuals' information can be misused to commit

---

[7] Exec. Order No. 13681, 79 Fed. Reg. 63491 (Oct. 23, 2014). See GAO, Digital Television Transition: Increased Federal Planning and Risk Management Could Further Facilitate the DTV Transition, GAO-08-43 (Washington, D.C.: Nov. 19, 2007); and Standards for Internal Control in the Federal Government, GAO-14-704G (Washington, D.C.: Sept. 10, 2014). Also see Office of Management and Budget, Preparing for and Responding to a Breach of Personally Identifiable Information, M-17-12 (Washington, D.C.: Jan. 3, 2017).

[8] Identity thieves can obtain sensitive personal information through various methods. For instance, thieves can use phishing to trick individuals or employees of an organization into sharing their own or others' sensitive personal information. Phishing uses authentic-looking, but fake, emails to request information from users or direct them to a fake website that requests information. Identity theft also can occur as a result of the loss or theft of data (a lost or stolen wallet or a thief digging through household trash). Some individuals may

United States Government Accountability Office

identity theft, fraud, or inflict other types of harm. Identity theft occurs when individuals' information is used without authorization in an attempt to commit fraud or other crimes. In 2016, according to the Bureau of Justice Statistics, an estimated 26 million people—10 percent of U.S. residents aged 16 or older—reported that they had been victims of identity theft in the previous year.[9] One potential source of identity theft is a data breach at an organization that maintains large amounts of sensitive personal information. Recent data breaches include the 2018 breach of Marriott International's Starwood guest registration database, which may have exposed information of millions of individuals, and the 2017 data breach at Equifax, Inc., a nationwide consumer reporting agency, which exposed identifying information of at least 145.5 million people.[10] The types of harm that can result from exposure of sensitive personal information include the following:

- Financial fraud from identity theft, which can include
  - o *new-account fraud*, in which thieves use identifying data, such as Social Security and driver's license numbers, to open new financial accounts without that person's knowledge; and,
  - o *existing-account fraud*, which is more common and entails the use or takeover of existing accounts, such as credit or debit card accounts, to make unauthorized charges or withdraw money.[11]

---

reveal sensitive information willingly, such as on social media accounts, which when combined with other information can allow fraudsters to steal identities.

[9] Department of Justice, Bureau of Justice Statistics, *Victims of Identity Theft, 2016* (Washington, D.C.: January 2019).

[10] We use "nationwide consumer reporting agency" to refer to the Fair Credit Reporting Act's term "consumer reporting agency that compiles and maintains files on consumers on a nationwide basis." The act defines such an agency as one that regularly engages in the practice of assembling or evaluating, and maintaining public record information and credit account information regarding consumers residing nationwide for the purpose of furnishing consumer reports to third parties bearing on a consumer's credit worthiness, credit standing, or credit capacity. 15 U.S.C. § 1681a(p). The three agencies that operate nationwide (Equifax, Experian, and TransUnion) provide reports commonly used to determine an individual's eligibility for credit, employment, and insurance.

[11] According to the Bureau of Justice Statistics, for 85 percent of identity-theft victims in 2016, the most recent incident involved misuse or attempted misuse of only one type of existing account, such as a credit card or bank account. Approximately 1 percent of those 16 or older experienced the opening of a new account or other misuse of personal information apart

Data Breaches

9

- o *Tax refund fraud,* which occurs when a Social Security number or other personally identifiable information is used to file a fraudulent tax return seeking a refund.[12]
- o *Government benefits fraud,* which occurs when thieves use stolen personal information to fraudulently obtain government benefits. For example, the Social Security Administration has reported that personal information of beneficiaries has been used to fraudulently redirect the beneficiary's direct deposit benefits.[13]
- o *Medical identity theft,* which occurs when someone uses an individual's name or personal identifying information to obtain medical services or prescription drugs fraudulently, including submitting fraudulent insurance claims.
- o *Synthetic identity theft,* which involves the creation of a fictitious identity, typically by using a combination of real data and fabricated information. The federal government has identified synthetic identity theft as an emerging trend.[14]
- o *Child identity theft,* which occurs when a child's Social Security number or other identifying information is stolen and used to commit fraudulent activity.

---

from misuse of an existing account. See Bureau of Justice Statistics, *Victims of Identity Theft, 2016.* While existing-account fraud is a significant problem, existing laws limit consumer liability for such fraud. As a matter of policy, some credit and debit card issuers may voluntarily cover all fraudulent charges. For example, for unauthorized credit card charges, cardholder liability is limited to a maximum of $50 per card. 15 U.S.C. § 1643; 12 C.F.R. § 1026.12. For unauthorized automated teller machine or debit card transactions, the Electronic Fund Transfer Act generally limits consumer liability, depending on how quickly the consumer reports the loss or theft of the card. *See* 15 U.S.C. § 1693g; 12 C.F.R. §1005.6.

[12] GAO, Identity Theft: IRS Needs to Strengthen Taxpayer Authentication Efforts, GAO-18-418 (Washington, D.C.: June 22, 2018).

[13] For a related GAO report, see Social Security Numbers: OMB Actions Needed to Strengthen Federal Efforts to Limit Identity Theft Risks by Reducing Collection, Use, and Display, GAO-17-553 (Washington, D.C.: July 25, 2017).

[14] GAO, Highlights of a Forum: Combating Synthetic Identity Fraud, GAO-17-708SP (Washington, D.C.: July 26, 2017). For example, individuals may face difficulties obtaining credit if their Social Security number has been used as part of a synthetic identity to commit fraud, or may face health risks if their records are connected to someone else. Synthetic identity fraud has grown significantly in recent years and resulted in significant financial losses to the financial industry and federal government.

United States Government Accountability Office

- o *Other types of fraud* that occur when personal information is used; for example, to set up mobile phone or utility accounts, or to engage in activities such as applying for employment or renting a home.
- The harms caused by exposure of personal information or identity theft can extend beyond tangible financial loss, including the following:
  - o *Lost time.* Victims of identity theft or fraud may spend significant amounts of time working to restore their identities. In 2016, according to the Bureau of Justice Statistics survey of identity victims, most victims resolved issues in 1 day or less but about 1 percent of victims spent 6 months or more resolving their identity theft issues.[15]
  - o *Emotional distress and reputational harm.* Exposed information also can cause emotional distress, a loss of privacy, or reputational injury. In 2016, according to the Bureau of Justice Statistics, about 10 percent of those who experienced identity theft reported suffering severe emotional distress.
  - o *Harm from state-based actors.* State-sponsored espionage can cause harm to individuals when nations use cyber tools as part of information-gathering, espionage, or other nefarious activities.

Consumers' Options to Address Risks or Harm

Options available to consumers to help prevent or mitigate identity theft include actions they can take on their own (generally for free) or services they can purchase.[16]

---

[15] Department of Justice, Bureau of Justice Statistics, *Victims of Identity Theft, 2016* (January 2019).

[16] See GAO-17-254 for additional details on these options.

Data Breaches 11

Actions individual consumers can take themselves include the following:

- *Placing a credit freeze.* A credit or security freeze restricts potential creditors from accessing a credit report until the consumer asks the agency to remove or temporarily lift the freeze.
- *Placing a fraud alert.* A fraud alert on a credit report requires businesses to verify a consumer's identity before they issue credit.
- *Monitoring accounts and other information.*[17]
  - o *Reviewing free annual credit reports.* Individuals can request one copy of their credit report every 12 months (available for free at AnnualCreditReport.com).from each of the three nationwide consumer reporting agencies.[18]
  - o *Reviewing financial statements and other accounts.* Individuals can review bank and other financial statements regularly for suspicious activity and make use of automatic transaction alerts and other free features that financial institutions offer to detect potential fraud. Individuals also can regularly review mobile phone or utility accounts for unusual activity.
  - o *Reviewing health insurance benefits explanations and medical information.* Individuals can review explanation-of-benefits statements from their health insurer to detect fraudulent insurance claims or monitor their files at their healthcare providers to detect unauthorized use of medical services.

Consumers also can obtain various free or fee-based *identity theft services*, which are commercial products that generally offer tools intended to help consumers detect identity theft and restore their identity if it has

---

[17] Department of Justice, Bureau of Justice Statistics, *Victims of Identity Theft, 2016* (January 2019).The survey found that the most common ways victims discovered identity theft was by being contacted by a financial institution (about 48 percent) or noticing fraudulent charges on an account (about 19 percent). About 1.4 percent of victims said they discovered the theft through a credit report or credit monitoring service.

[18] Individuals can use other mechanisms to request and review credit reports from other consumer reporting agencies every year for free.

12 *United States Government Accountability Office*

been compromised. The private research firm IBISWorld estimated that the U.S. market for identity theft services was about $3billion annually in 2015–2017.[19] The services may be marketed directly to individuals for a monthly or annual fee. In addition, private- and public-sector entities that have experienced data breaches sometimes purchase these services and offer them to affected individuals at no cost.[20]

- Identity theft services most often include
  - o *credit monitoring*, which tracks an individual's credit reports and sends alerts about potentially suspicious activity;
  - o *identity monitoring*, which aims to monitor other sources such as public records and illicit websites (sometimes referred to as the "dark web");
  - o *identity restoration*, which provides a range of services to recover from identity theft; and
  - o *identity theft insurance*, which reimburses individuals for certain costs related to the process of restoring identities.

Other actions consumers can take to protect their identity include adoption of certain data security practices and early filing of tax returns. Data security practices can help protect sensitive information. For example, individuals can change or avoid sharing or re-using passwords, and make use of strong passwords and authentication options on online accounts; properly safeguard or shred sensitive paper documents; and limit access to their sensitive information on social media. Filing a tax return early reduces the risk of tax refund fraud, and some victims of tax refund fraud may be eligible for an Identity Protection Personal Identification Number (PIN)—issued by the Internal Revenue Service IRS)—to prevent future fraud. To protect their Social Security benefits, individuals can set

---

[19] See IBISWorld, *Identity Theft Protection Services in the US:* Industry Market Research Report. We cited the reports published in April 2015 and April 2016 in GAO-17-254; and accessed the August 2017 report at https://www.ibisworld.com/industry-trends/specialized-market-research-reports/technology/computer-services/identity-theft-protection-services.html, on August 30, 2018.

[20] For example, in response to breaches of its databases in 2015, OPM offered identity theft services to approximately 22 million people affected by the breaches.

up an online account at the Social Security Administration to monitor their benefits accounts.

Limited Information Is Available on Effectiveness of Options after Data Breaches, but Credit Freezes Can Prevent New-Account Fraud

We did not identify any studies that analyzed whether consumers who sign up for or purchase identity theft services encounter fewer instances of identity theft or detect instances of financial or other fraud more—or less—rapidly than consumers who take steps on their own. Views of experts varied, but most said identity theft services have limitations and would not address all data breach risks. Most experts also said that a credit freeze, which consumers place on their own for free, is a useful way to prevent one type of financial fraud—the illegal opening of new credit accounts in consumers' names. Based on our review and discussions with experts, consumers can consider four factors when deciding on options to address risks after a data breach: the extent to which an option might prevent fraud; the cost of an option; its convenience; and the type of information that was exposed and may be at risk.

No Independent Research Assesses Effectiveness of Consumer Options to Address Risks after Data Breaches

Information that can help consumers assess their options for mitigating and addressing the risks of identity theft and other harm from data breaches is limited. Specifically, we did not identify any studies that analyzed whether consumers who sign up for free or purchase identity theft services encounter fewer instances of identity theft or detect instances of financial or other fraud more—or less—rapidly than consumers who take steps on

14   *United States Government Accountability Office*

their own for free—such as monitoring their credit reports or placing a credit freeze. For consumers who experienced identity theft, we did not find any studies that compared the effectiveness of free options to help consumers recover from identity theft with commercial identity restoration services. In addition to searching databases of scholarly publications and other sources, a range of academic, consumer, government, and industry experts we interviewed told us that they were unaware of any specific independent studies on the effectiveness of consumer options.[21]

We interviewed representatives of seven companies that provide identity theft services about how they assess the effectiveness of their services and found that what they measure does not directly address how effective these services would be in mitigating the risks of identity theft compared with options consumers can take on their own. For example, two company representatives said that their services focus on detection of fraudulent activity or assistance after identity theft has occurred, rather than on prevention of identity theft or other harms. The representatives of each of the providers said that their companies generally measure how customers use their products and services; customer satisfaction (for example, through surveys or other feedback); and whether the products work as intended (for example, whether alerts of fraudulent activity are successfully delivered to customers or customers can successfully access the company's website when they need to). Companies that offer identity restoration services also measure the rate at which they complete the process of recovering stolen identities. While it is not possible to prevent

---

[21] See Vyacheslav Mikhed and Michael Vogan, *How Data Breaches Affect Consumer Credit* (Philadelphia, Penn.: November 2017). The study used the 2012 South Carolina Department of Revenue data breach as a natural experiment to study how data breaches and news coverage about them affect consumers' interactions with the credit market and their use of credit. The study found that some consumers directly exposed to the breach protected themselves against potential losses from future fraudulent use of stolen information by monitoring their files and freezing access to their credit reports. The response of consumers only exposed to news about the breach was negligible. As part of their analysis, the researchers measured the extent to which affected individuals signed up for credit monitoring services, credit freezes, fraud alerts, or opted out of receiving prescreened offers of credit. The study found that the most frequent options chosen were credit monitoring services and credit freezes. The researchers also found that more individuals opted to place freezes on their credit reports than the researchers had predicted.

Data Breaches 15

identity fraud, four representatives said that early detection of fraud is important as it allows consumers to address potential fraud more quickly.

FTC, a primary source for assistance to consumers on issues related to data breaches and identity theft, has advised consumers that the effectiveness of services that offer identity monitoring depends on factors such as the kinds of databases the service provider monitors, how well the databases collect information, and how often the service provider checks each database.[22] For example, FTC suggests that consumers ask if service providers check databases that show payday loan applications or changes in addresses for misuse of their information as part of identity monitoring. In reviewing consumer education and promotional materials on the websites of five identity theft service companies we contacted that offer identity monitoring, we found that three providers included information about which types of databases they monitor; the other two did not.[23]

Government and commercial entities—such as federal agencies and retail stores—that decide to purchase identity theft services to offer to affected individuals after a breach of their data do not necessarily base their decision on how effective these services are. Rather, according to industry and some government representatives we interviewed, some base their decisions on federal or state legal requirements to offer such services and the expectations of affected customers or employees for some action on the breached entities' part. Representatives of retail and banking associations we interviewed indicated that it has become the industry standard to offer 1 year of credit or identity monitoring services in the wake of a data breach. One industry representative said that in some cases the decision is not based on the effectiveness of the services.[24] States such as California require

---

[22] Federal Trade Commission, *Consumer Information: Identity Theft Protection Services*, https://www.consumer.ftc.gov/articles/0235-identity-theft-protection-services; accessed on July 10, 2018.

[23] We reported in 2017 that the Consumer Federation of America offers guidance to individuals and entities on selecting identity theft service providers: Consumer Federation of America, *Best Practices for Identity Theft Services, Version 2.0* (Washington, D.C.: Nov. 17, 2015).

[24] Once exposed, there is no time limit on the potential for identity thieves to use such information to commit fraud.

16　　　*United States Government Accountability Office*

companies to offer some type of identity theft service after a data breach.[25] Moreover, Connecticut requires health insurers and certain health care-related companies to offer identity theft services following an actual or suspected data breach. In 2017, we reported that companies do not assess the effectiveness of an identity theft provider's services when selecting a vendor to provide such services. Rather, they consider other selection factors, including price, reputation, capacity to respond quickly to large-scale breaches, and ability to provide comprehensive post-breach services, such as complying with statutory notification requirements. But companies that purchase identity theft services may be in a position to obtain more detailed information from potential providers than is publicly available to consumers.

Views of Experts Varied, but Most Said Identity Theft Services Have Limitations and Would Not Address All Data Breach Risks

In the absence of independent evidence of the effectiveness of identity theft mitigation options, we interviewed representatives and reviewed consumer education materials, working papers, and articles from academic, consumer, industry, and government entities. No one solution can protect against the full range of risks to individuals whose personal information was exposed in a data breach, based on our review of documentation and the views of academic, consumer, government, and industry experts. We obtained perspectives on the value of options available to consumers. The following summarizes key observations:

Identity Theft Services

Representatives of 9 of the 10 consumer groups we interviewed generally viewed credit or identity monitoring (or both) to be of limited

---

[25] Massachusetts enacted a law in 2019 that requires companies that experience a breach in which Social Security numbers are disclosed, or reasonably believed to have been disclosed, to offer credit monitoring services at no cost for at least 18 months, or 42 months if the company is a consumer reporting agency, among other things.

value. However, one consumer group representative noted that identity monitoring might be useful in circumstances in which Social Security numbers were compromised. In addition, a few consumer group representatives indicated that consumers could consider signing up for such services if they are offered for free. If identity theft services are not free, FTC and CFPB consumer education materials recommend that consumers consider the benefits and limitations of such services and compare them to free or low-cost options before signing up. A few consumer groups and one academic highlighted that consumers may not fully understand the limitations of signing up for identity theft services. A few consumer group representatives and one industry and state government representative cautioned that free services may be offered for only 1 or 2 years; exposed information can be used for identity theft or other harms over a much longer period. For example, in 2017, we reported that nation-state actors that steal consumer data as part of their espionage activities can wait much longer than a private identity thief to use compromised information (if at all), according to one identity theft service provider. In addition, CFPB consumer information and a few consumer group representatives noted that consumers should be aware that some services may try to charge consumers after the free period ends.

Some consumer group and one industry representatives also said that the value of one feature of identity monitoring—dark web monitoring—is unclear. One representative said that there is nothing new that consumers can do once they learn their information was found on an illicit website. Rather, they must continue to monitor their accounts as they already should have been doing. In addition, one consumer group representative indicated that these services may provide consumers with a false sense of security.

Experts we interviewed for our 2017 report said that identity restoration in particular could be helpful to consumers. FTC staff and one consumer group representative we interviewed said that one-on-one assistance can be helpful. Identity restoration typically is included with other identity theft services rather than offered as a stand-alone service. However, the level of service provided in identity restoration can vary substantially—some providers offer individualized hands-on assistance, while others largely

18 *United States Government Accountability Office*

provide self-help information that is of more limited value. In our 2017 report, we also found that another feature of identity theft services, identity theft insurance, may provide minimal benefits for consumers. More details about identity theft insurance appear later in this report.

Options to Prevent Fraud or Harm Unrelated to Credit Accounts

Consumers have limited options to mitigate risks of other harms from data breaches, such as medical identity theft and identity theft tax refund fraud. Commercial identity theft services, credit freezes, and fraud alerts do not directly address these risks. Some consumer, government, and industry representatives cited self-monitoring as a way for consumers to be on the alert for these other types of fraud.

Consistent with our 2017 report, identity theft service providers we interviewed generally indicated that their products and services do not directly monitor for these types of fraud. However, two noted that they would assist with any identity restoration involving medical identity theft, tax refund fraud, or government benefits fraud (such as fraudulently redirecting Social Security benefits). Identity theft services also may address these types of fraud indirectly—for example, detecting a fraudulent change of address can prevent sensitive health insurance information from being redirected to the fraudster. A few consumer groups said that consumers may not understand which risks commercial identity theft services address. Additionally, we reported in 2017 that identity theft services do not address non-financial harms, such as emotional distress, embarrassment, and harm to one's reputation. For example, a House Committee report on the OPM data breaches noted that the information stolen from background investigations included some of the most intimate and potentially embarrassing aspects of a person's life, such as mental health history, misuse of alcohol or drugs, or problems with gambling.[26] Identity theft services also may be of limited value in cases of nation-state espionage. For example, in 2017, we reported that when the source of the

---

[26] The OPM Data Breach: How the Government Jeopardized Our National Security for More than a Generation, House Committee on Oversight and Government Reform, 114th Congress (Sept. 7, 2016).

Data Breaches

19

data breach appears to be a nation state (as opposed to a private party), the risk of the information being sold for monetary purposes is likely to be lower, according to an FTC representative.

Importance of Data Security

In the view of some experts, entities such as the federal government and private companies that hold consumer data have a responsibility to protect those data.[27] A few experts said that the burden should not be on consumers to protect data they do not control. Except in certain circumstances, companies are generally not required to be transparent about the consumer data they hold or how they collect, maintain, use, and secure these data.[28] Identity theft service providers may contract with third parties such as consumer reporting agencies or with third-party identity monitoring providers, such as dark web monitoring services. Moreover, one consumer group representative noted that identity monitoring services require consumers to provide additional personal information to enroll—which also could be compromised if the service provider's information were breached.

Finally, consumer group and government researchers we interviewed suggested other options that entities can (or already) use to address risks of harm. For example, one government researcher noted that financial institutions have started to use multifactor authentication and other technologies that can help institutions verify a consumer's identity and thus help prevent fraud. Multifactor authentication involves first logging into an online account using the traditional username and password, and then the institution sending a verification code to a mobile phone or e-mail address that the consumer must enter as part of the log-in process. In addition, one

---

[27] We previously reported on data security and data protection at entities that store sensitive personal information. See GAO, Data Protection: Actions Taken by Equifax and Federal Agencies in Response to the 2017 Breach, GAO-18-559 (Washington, D.C.: Aug. 30, 2018); and Consumer Data Protection: Actions Needed to Strengthen Oversight of Consumer Reporting Agencies, GAO-19-196 (Washington, D.C.; Feb. 21, 2019).

[28] See GAO, Information Resellers: Consumer Privacy Framework Needs to Reflect Changes in the Technology and the Marketplace, GAO-13-663 (Washington, D.C.: Sept. 25, 2013); and Personal Information: Key Federal Privacy Laws Do Not Require Information Resellers to Safeguard All Sensitive Data, GAO-06-674 (Washington, D.C.: June 26, 2006).

20 *United States Government Accountability Office*

researcher noted that some institutions have started to use facial recognition technology, or to ask an account holder to provide answers to questions such as the size of the account holder's last deposit.[29] Other biometric technologies such as fingerprint recognition on mobile phones, or one-time passcodes that are synced with financial institutions' websites, also can help, according to one researcher and one consumer group representative. Other strategies can focus on reducing the riskiness of breaches by making information less useful for purposes of committing identity theft. For example, one researcher noted that organizations could encrypt data or use tokens so static account numbers could not be used on their own. There is no single solution to address all risks of harm, based on our review of documentation and the views of academic, consumer, government, and industry experts.

Consumers Can Use Free Credit Freezes and Fraud Alerts to Effectively Prevent New-Account Fraud

A credit freeze is the only consumer option that can prevent one type of identity theft-related fraud, and recent federal legislation made credit freezes free and easier to place or lift. This option is effective because it restricts potential creditors from accessing a consumer's credit report to open a new account until the consumer asks the nationwide consumer reporting agency to remove or temporarily lift the freeze. In contrast, identity theft services and self-monitoring detect or remediate identity theft after it has occurred, but do not prevent the fraud from occurring in the first place. We interviewed representatives, or reviewed the consumer education or informational materials, of consumer, industry, and government entities and found that almost all of them included credit freezes on credit reports as a useful consumer option to protect against identity theft.

---

[29] Facial recognition technology is one of several biometric technologies that identify individuals by measuring and analyzing their physiological or behavioral characteristics.

More specifically, the Economic Growth, Regulatory Relief, and Consumer Protection Act, which took effect on September 21, 2018, required the three nationwide consumer reporting agencies (Equifax, Experian, and TransUnion) to make placing and lifting freezes free and specifies that the agencies must place a freeze within 1 business day, and lift it within 1 hour, of receiving a telephone or electronic request (see fig. 1).[30] Consumers must contact each of the three agencies individually and request the freeze. Consumers obtain a PIN from each company, which enables them to lift or remove a freeze at a later date. Before the 2018 act, consumers typically had to pay $5-$10 per agency to place a credit freeze. Some experts had noted cost and inconvenience as some of the limitations to a credit freeze. The new law addresses these concerns to some degree by making credit freezes free and requiring these consumer reporting agencies to lift freezes expeditiously on request.

While the new law removed some barriers to placing credit freezes, others still exist and the freezes have some limitations. For example, consumers still have to lift a freeze before applying for a loan or new credit account and need to place or remove a freeze at each consumer reporting agency separately, which could cause delays for consumers actively shopping for a home, car, or other purchase requiring the extension of credit. Two consumer groups said that there is confusion about how the law would affect minor children. (Under the new law, credit freezes only can be placed on behalf of children under age 16, but not minors ages 16 and 17—who must place freezes themselves).

Moreover, as the new law only applies to the three nationwide consumer reporting agencies, credit freezes do not protect against new-account fraud resulting from the use of credit reports from other consumer reporting agencies.

---

[30] *See* Pub. L. No. 115-174, §301, 132 Stat. 1296, 1326 (2018) (codified at 15 U.S.C. § 1681c–1(i)).The Congressional Budget Office estimated that about 0.3 percent of Americans with credit reports have frozen their credit. Congressional Budget Office, *Congressional Budget Office Cost Estimate, S. 2155, Economic Growth, Regulatory Relief, and Consumer Protection Act* (Washington, D.C.: March 5, 2018).

Selected 2018 Federal Legislative Changes

Free Credit Freezes
- Individuals can place freezes on their credit reports for **free** at the three nationwide consumer reporting agencies—Equifax, Experian, and TransUnion.

Freeze within 1 Business Day
- Consumer reporting agency must place the freeze within **1 business day** of receiving a phone or electronic request (or within **3 business days** of a mailed request).

Unfreeze within 1 Hour
- Consumer reporting agency must remove a freeze within **1 hour** of receiving a phone or electronic request (or within **3 business days** of a mailed request).

Why Credit Freezes Can Be Helpful:
- Prevents new accounts from being opened, in situations where review of a credit report is required.
- Guardians can place credit freezes for minor children (under age 16) or adults who are incapacitated.
- Cited by experts as one of the most effective tools for preventing new-account fraud.
- Relatively convenient: freezes can be managed electronically (or through other methods) and can be removed temporarily for a specified duration.

Consumers Should Be Aware:
- Consumers must request a freeze at each of the three agencies separately.
- Could still cause delays in approval of loans or other credit applications, especially if consumer forgets or loses the personal information number (PIN) the agencies give to consumers to unfreeze their credit reports.
- Freezes do not prevent fraud on existing accounts (for example, the use of a stolen credit card number to make charges on a credit card).
- Does not prevent other types of harm, such as tax refund or medical identity fraud.
- Not all access to credit reports is frozen (for example, still allowed for insurance underwriting and employment background checks).
- Credit reports at agencies other than Equifax, Experian, and TransUnion will not be frozen (for example, those used to open utility accounts).

Source: GAO analysis, Federal Trade Communication, Consumer Financial Protection Bureau, and consumer and industry organizations. | GAO-19-230.

Figure 1. Overview of Credit Freezes.

For example, one consumer group recommended that consumers place a fourth freeze with the National Consumer Telecom and Utilities Exchange—a consumer reporting agency that maintains credit reports that telecommunications or utilities companies may use to check the creditworthiness of consumers interested in opening phone or utility accounts. The law also permits insurance companies and employers to continue to access credit reports even after they are frozen, among other exceptions.

One general limitation of credit freezes is that they do not protect against new-account fraud in cases in which credit reports are not used to verify a consumer's creditworthiness. Furthermore, credit freezes do not

Data Breaches

protect against existing-account fraud, such as fraudulent credit card charges, or certain other types of fraud, such as identity theft tax refund fraud or synthetic identity fraud using elements of individuals' identity information.

While experts with whom we spoke across industry, government, and consumer groups generally believed credit freezes to be an effective tool in preventing new-account fraud, some consumer and industry experts indicated that fraud alerts also can be a good alternative for consumers. Unlike a credit freeze, a fraud alert still allows companies to access an individual's credit report for the purpose of opening a loan or credit account. Fraud alerts notify companies requesting the reports that the individual may have been a victim of identity theft. The alerts require companies to verify consumers' identities before they issue credit to a consumer.[31] Fraud alerts therefore can make it harder for an identity thief to open accounts in a consumer's name. Moreover, fraud alerts are easier to place than credit freezes, as consumers only need to contact one of the three nationwide consumer reporting agencies to place a fraud alert (that agency is then obligated to contact the other two on the individual's behalf). The Economic Growth, Regulatory Relief, and Consumer Protection Act extended the period of an initial fraud alert from 90 days to 1 year.[32]

However, fraud alerts do not restrict access to consumers' credit reports the way freezes do. Therefore, some consumer group and industry representatives noted that consumers should be aware that a fraud alert may not offer as strong a protection as a credit freeze does. We did not find

---

[31] *See* 15 U.S.C. § 1681c-1(h)(1)(B). Consumers can request an initial fraud alert, extended fraud alert, or active duty alert at no cost with any one of the three nationwide consumer reporting agencies, which automatically must notify the other two. *See* 15 U.S.C. § 1681c-1(a)-(c). An initial fraud alert stays on the victim's credit file for 1 year after which the consumer may place another fraud alert. An extended fraud alert, which lasts for 7 years, is available to victims of identity theft who have filed a formal identity theft report with one of the three agencies. Active duty alerts, which last for 1 year, are available to deployed military service members.

[32] See Pub. L. No. 115-174, §301(a)(1), 132 Stat. 1296, 1326 (2018) (codified at 15 U.S.C. § 1681c–1(a)(1)(a)). Additionally, the act mandated that FTC issue a rule regarding the law's requirement that the nationwide consumer reporting agencies provide a free electronic credit monitoring service that would notify active-duty military members within 24 hours of any "material" additions or modifications to their credit files. § 302(d)(1).

24   *United States Government Accountability Office*

any data or analysis on the effectiveness of fraud alerts compared to credit freezes or monitoring options. One consumer group told us that it recommends that after a data breach consumers first place a fraud alert, because it requires contacting only one of the three nationwide consumer reporting agencies, and then follow up by placing a credit freeze at the three agencies.

The three nationwide consumer reporting agencies also offer a product called a credit lock that is functionally similar to a credit freeze in that it restricts access to an individual's credit report. Credit locks do not require consumers to use a PIN and consumers can turn access to credit reports on or off through an application on their mobile phone. However, credit locks are not subject to the same federal requirements regarding the placement and removal of freezes and therefore do not offer the same degree of protection to consumers.[33] Instead, credit locks are private products subject to the consumer reporting agencies' terms and conditions, which could change. A credit lock is in place only as long as the individual subscribes to an agency's service, but a credit freeze remains in place until the consumer chooses to remove it. Finally, consumers may be charged a fee to place a credit lock, whereas credit freezes can now be placed for free.

Factors Consumers Can Consider When Assessing Options after Data Breaches

Based on our interviews and review of consumer education materials and our 2017 report, we identified four factors that consumers can consider in deciding which options are best for them in responding to a breach of their personal information:

---

[33] The Fair Credit Reporting Act protects the accuracy and confidentiality of personal information collected or used for eligibility determinations for such purposes as credit, insurance, or employment. As such, it regulates the collection and use of consumers' personal information by consumer reporting agencies. Moreover, the Fair Credit Reporting Act requires information on credit freezes to be included in any notice of consumer rights required under the act. *See* 15 U.S.C. § 1681c-1(i)(5).

Data Breaches 25

- *Prevention.* Consumers can consider the extent to which an option might prevent fraud. For example, because credit freezes block all access to an individual's credit report, by definition they are effective in preventing new-account fraud where credit reports are used as part of the account-opening process. Identity theft services do not prevent fraud, but detect suspicious activity or help restore identities after identity theft.

- *Cost.* Consumers can consider the cost of a service. For instance, consumers can consider whether to pay for commercial identity theft services if they believe the value of the service outweighs the effort of monitoring their accounts on their own. In addition, they may consider that credit freezes now are available for free.

- *Convenience.* Consumers may consider the convenience of a service. For example, while consumers can monitor their own credit reports and accounts, some might prefer not to or may be limited in their ability to do so. In addition, technologies offered through financial institutions that automatically alert customers to any transactions involving their accounts can be a convenient, no-cost way for consumers to monitor their accounts.

- *Type of information at risk.* Finally, several experts from consumer and industry organizations indicated that the type of option that might be beneficial would depend on the type of information at risk. For example, one consumer group representative noted that if a credit card number were stolen, an identity monitoring service that monitored the dark web for Social Security numbers might not be needed. Furthermore, consumers should consider that credit monitoring will be of limited effectiveness in alerting them to misuse of an existing credit account—which is more common than fraud related to setting up new accounts.[34] For more information on consumers' options, see appendix II.

---

[34] As noted previously, for 85 percent of identity-theft victims in 2016, the most recent incident involved misuse or attempted misuse of one type of existing account, such as a credit card or bank account. Only 1 percent of those 16 or older experienced the opening of a new account or other misuse of personal information apart from misuse of an existing account.

26 *United States Government Accountability Office*

FEDERAL AGENCIES PROVIDE ASSISTANCE TO CONSUMERS AFFECTED BY DATA BREACHES AND IDENTITY THEFT

Among federal agencies, FTC serves as a primary source for free assistance (including online resources, educational outreach, and customized assistance through IdentityTheft.gov) to consumers on ways to respond to data breaches, identity theft, and related harm. Approximately 13 percent of those affected by the 2015 OPM breaches used credit and identity monitoring and identity restoration services that OPM offered them and a fraction of a percent made identity theft insurance claims (the payouts for which averaged $1,800). Data we assessed for this report support a 2017 recommendation we made to the Office of Management and Budget (OMB) to revise guidance to federal agencies about responding to data breaches and one to Congress to consider permitting agencies to determine appropriate levels of identity theft insurance offered after data breaches.

FTC Is Primary Provider of Federal Assistance to Consumers Affected by Data Breaches and Identity Theft

Federal Trade Commission

FTC, as a primary source for assistance to consumers on issues related to data breaches and identity theft, provides guidance and assistance through its website and through conferences and workshops.[35]

See Department of Justice, Bureau of Justice Statistics, *Victims of Identity Theft, 2016* (January 2019).

[35] The Identity Theft and Assumption Deterrence Act of 1998 establishes FTC as the central clearinghouse for identity theft victim complaints and directs FTC to provide consumer education to identity theft victims. *See* Pub. L. No. 105-318, § 5(a), 112 Stat. 3007, 3010 (codified at 18 U.S.C. § 1028 note). More recently, an Executive Order included a provision calling for federal agencies to centralize identity theft information and resources at FTC's website, IdentityTheft.gov, and through the general FTC website. Exec. Order No. 13681, 78 Fed. Reg. 63491, 63492 (Oct. 23, 2014). FTC's primary legal authority comes from

Online and Printed Resources

FTC's home page includes links to identity theft-related resources, including information about key options consumers can consider to help them mitigate identity theft risks and other harms, and a link to IdentityTheft.gov (discussed later in this section). FTC updates the information regularly, such as after large-scale data breaches.

Outreach

FTC maintains relationships with state government, law enforcement, and community and consumer organizations, through which it conducts outreach about how to respond to exposure or loss of personal information and identity theft mitigation. For example, FTC collaborated with the International Association of the Chiefs of Police to update the association's model policy for identity theft to include referral information for IdentityTheft.gov. FTC also has held webinars, conferences, and workshops on topics related to data breaches and identity theft for groups including government officials, nonprofits, and the general public.

Customized Assistance (IdentityTheft.gov)

FTC provides information and customized assistance through IdentityTheft.gov to individuals whose information was lost or stolen or who experienced identity theft or other harm, such as tax refund fraud. During fiscal year 2018, IdentityTheft.gov received almost 2 million unique visitors. The website in its current form has been in place since January 2016 and offers the following types of assistance:

---

section 5 of the Federal Trade Commission Act, which prohibits unfair or deceptive acts or practices in the marketplace. *See* 15 U.S.C. § 45. FTC has authority to enforce sector-specific laws, including the Truth in Lending Act, the CANSPAM Act, the Children's Online Privacy Protection Act, the Equal Credit Opportunity Act, the Fair Credit Reporting Act, the Fair Debt Collection Practices Act, and the Telemarketing and Consumer Fraud and Abuse Prevention Act. As directed by Congress, FTC also has authority to issue rules that regulate specific areas of consumer privacy and security. For example, FTC's Red Flags Rule requires financial institutions and certain creditors to have programs to identify, detect, and respond to patterns, practices, or specific activities that could indicate identity theft.

28   *United States Government Accountability Office*

- *Steps to take after identity theft. IdentityTheft.gov* provides individual victims with step-by-step instructions to resolve specific problems. From January 2016 (when FTC launched the current version of IdentityTheft.gov) through October 1, 2018, approximately 700,000 individuals set up and activated accounts on the website to help them recover from identity theft. Individuals who set up accounts can indicate what kind of information was stolen and what kind of adverse event they experienced. The site helps users generate pre-filled letters, affidavits, and forms to send to consumer reporting agencies, businesses, debt collectors, and IRS, as appropriate. For example, individuals who fill out an Identity Theft Report affidavit can use this report instead of filing a police report to request extended 7- year fraud alerts (available to identity theft victims) on their credit reports. In addition, individuals who experienced tax refund fraud can fill out a form on IdentityTheft.gov that is then submitted directly to IRS. An individual who experienced credit card fraud would be advised to take different steps than one who experienced fraud related to utility bills or medical insurance.
- *Steps to take after data breaches or loss of personal information.* IdentityTheft.gov/databreach provides checklists and suggestions for people whose personal information was lost or exposed but has not yet been misused.

FTC also maintains an online chat function and telephone number for those who need additional assistance. For complex cases, FTC staff may refer individuals to the Identity Theft Resource Center, a nonprofit organization.

We found that in developing and updating the website, FTC followed some key practices for consumer education planning.[36] One key practice we identified was consulting with stakeholders. According to FTC staff we interviewed and documentation we reviewed, FTC obtained feedback from

---

[36] In GAO-08-43, we describe key practices for conducting consumer education identified by an expert panel that we convened.

stakeholders such as law enforcement agencies and community organizations in developing IdentityTheft.gov. Another key practice we identified was assessing users' needs. FTC conducted usability testing to ensure the site's features were easy to use. FTC staff also told us that after receiving user feedback, they made it easier for users to set up an account. FTC also made changes to IdentityTheft.gov—such as incorporating the ability to auto-generate forms—to implement a 2014 Executive Order calling for federal agencies to centralize identity theft information at the website.[37] Furthermore, in January 2018, FTC implemented a new function that allows users who report identity theft tax refund fraud to file reports directly with IRS. Since its launch in early 2018 through October 1, 2018, almost 22,000 IRS Identity Theft Affidavits (IRS Form 14039) were submitted to IRS through IdentityTheft.gov. In general, experts across consumer, government, and industry organizations and identity theft service providers we interviewed expressed the view that IdentityTheft.gov is a valuable or user-friendly resource.

Other Federal Agency Resources

Other federal agencies provide assistance to consumers on topics related to identity theft, including CFPB, the Department of Justice, IRS, and the Social Security Administration.[38]

CFPB. CFPB enforces, supervises for compliance with, and issues regulations to implement the federal consumer financial laws that address certain firms' and financial institutions' practices, which may include data security. A few of these laws and regulations contain provisions that can

---

[37] Exec. Order No. 13681, 78 Fed. Reg. 63491 (Oct. 23, 2014).

[38] For example, see Department of Justice, Identity Theft, https://www.justice.gov/criminal-fraud/identity-theft/identity-theft-and-identity-fraud, which we accessed on November 19, 2018. Also see Internal Revenue Service, *Taxpayer Guide to Identity Theft,* https://www.irs.gov/newsroom/taxpayer-guide-to-identity-theft, accessed on November 19, 2018; *Data Breach: Tax-Related Information for Taxpayers*, May 2018; and *Identity Protection: Prevention, Detection, and Victim Assistance,* July 2018. See Social Security Administration, *Identity Theft and Your Social Security Number.* These agencies were outside the scope of our review for this report, but we previously reported on some related topics (for instance, see GAO-18-418).

30   *United States Government Accountability Office*

help protect the personal information of consumers.[39] CFPB also offers consumer education resources.

Similarly to FTC, CFPB included information about how consumers can address risks related to exposure of personal information and recover from identity theft in the bureau's overall consumer education activities. CFPB provides consumer education materials related to data breaches and identity theft through its blog and its financial education resource, "Ask CFPB." CFPB also maintains relationships with external groups, such as librarian networks. CFPB provides links to FTC resources about data breaches and identity theft topics on its website, so as not to duplicate efforts, according to CFPB staff.[40] The two agencies also have coordinated some efforts. FTC and CFPB published a jointly produced blog post on September 21, 2018, the date the new free credit freeze and 1-year fraud alert provisions took effect. Such coordination is consistent with the 2014 Executive Order, which designated FTC as a centralized source of information about identity theft across the federal government.

Staff of both agencies said that in developing new resources, they monitor information from a variety of sources, including consumer complaints, news and social media, and reports from other government entities, law enforcement, or nongovernmental stakeholders.

Other Federal and State Agencies

IRS and the Social Security Administration provide some assistance to consumers for specific types of identity theft. For example, as noted previously, IRS provides some taxpayers with PINs if they are victims of

---

[39] These include sections 502 through 509 of the Gramm-Leach Bliley Act, sections 1031 and 1036 of the Dodd-Frank Wall Street Reform and Consumer Protection Act concerning unfair, deceptive, or abusive acts and practices, the Fair Credit Reporting Act, and the Fair Debt Collection Practices Act. *See* Pub. L. No. 111-203, § 1002(12), 124 Stat. 1376, 1957 (2010) (codified at 12 U.S.C. § 5481(12)). CFPB has no authority under section 501(b) of the Gramm-Leach Bliley Act, which required FTC and other agencies (but not CFPB) to establish standards for financial institutions on administrative, technical, and physical safeguards to ensure the security and confidentiality of customer records and information, to protect against anticipated threats or hazards to the security or integrity of such records, and protect against unauthorized access to or use of such records or information that could result in substantial harm or inconvenience to any customer. *See* 15 U.S.C. § 6801(b).

[40] Other federal agencies' websites also provide links to FTC resources, including those of OPM, IRS, the Department of Justice, and the Social Security Administration.

Data Breaches 31

identity theft tax refund fraud. In addition, states enforce laws and regulations and provide consumer education resources and assistance to consumers at risk of identity theft and other harms as a result of data breaches. For example, the Illinois Attorney General's office maintains a call-in number for victims of identity theft, and the Colorado Bureau of Investigation can assist residents with identity theft issues.

Few People Used Identity Theft Services OPM Provided, Very Few Made Insurance Claims, and Payouts Received Were Low

OPM offered identity theft services to approximately 22.1 million individuals whose personal information was compromised during the 2015 data breaches at OPM.[41] Personnel records or OPM systems containing information from the background investigations of current, former, and prospective federal employees and other individuals were breached. The services, offered at no cost to affected individuals, included credit monitoring, identity monitoring, identity restoration services, and identity theft insurance.[42] To receive credit and identity monitoring services, affected people have to enroll with the identity theft service provider with which OPM contracted, but identity theft insurance and identity theft restoration services are available to the entire affected population whether or not they enroll.

Few affected individuals have used the services. According to data from OPM, as of September 30, 2018, close to 3 million, or 13 percent, of individuals affected by the 2015 incidents had made use of the services. As seen in figure 2, the great majority of enrollments occurred in the months

---

[41] The federal contracts awarded in 2015 for the OPM data breaches provided for federal agencies to receive information about the identity theft services delivered by contractors, such as information about call-center wait times and the number and status of identity restoration cases.

[42] The identity restoration and insurance provided to consumers covers all incidents of identity theft that occur during the coverage period, regardless of the source.

immediately following notification of the breach.[43] OPM staff said that the spike in enrollments in July and August 2016 likely was due to the follow-up mailing that OPM sent to approximately 10 percent of affected individuals whose mailing addresses were incorrect in the original mailing of notifications.[44]

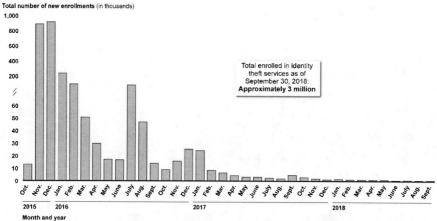

Source: GAO analysis of Office of Personnel Management data. | GAO-19-230.

Notes: The Office of Personnel Management (OPM) offered identity theft services to approximately 22.1 million individuals whose sensitive personal information was compromised during the 2015 data breaches of OPM personnel records or OPM systems containing information from the background investigations of current, former, and prospective federal employees and other individuals. The services included credit and identity monitoring, identity restoration services, and identity theft insurance. According to OPM staff, the spike in enrollments in July and August of 2016 likely was due to the follow-up mailing that OPM sent to approximately 10 percent of affected individuals whose mailing addresses were incorrect in the original September 2015 notification.

Figure 2. Enrollment in Identity Theft Services Offered by Office of Personnel Management, October 2015–September 2018.

---

[43] OPM data show that of the approximately 3 million individuals enrolled in identity theft services through September 30, 2018, there were about 2.7 million adults and 350,000 minors. See GAO-17-254 for more information.

[44] OPM worked with the Department of Defense and a commercial address validation service to identify the correct addresses and sent out notifications to these individuals in June 2016.

Data Breaches 33

In addition, according to OPM-reported data we reviewed, of the 3 million individuals who used the services, about 1 percent made identity restoration requests and a fraction of 1 percent submitted insurance claims. According to data we reviewed, approximately 27,000 identity restoration cases had been resolved as of September 30, 2018. In addition, 61 insurance claims (of 81 submitted) had been paid, totaling $112,000, with an average payout of $1,800.[45]

Since 2015, OPM has obligated approximately $421 million for identity theft services and as of November 30, 2018, OPM paid out approximately$361 million of the obligated funds.[46] OPM is required to provide identity theft services through September 2026.[47] The contract to provide these services on behalf of OPM expired in December 2018; OPM re-competed and awarded a single contract that month to ID Experts, the company that had been providing these services.[48]

After the OPM breaches in 2015, OPM provided federal employees and other affected individuals with information and guidance about their options in mailed letters and on its website. On its website, OPM developed a Cybersecurity Resource Center and included background about the breaches and who was affected; instructions for how to enroll in identity theft services; and a Frequently Asked Questions webpage that included links to FTC resources, including IdentityTheft.gov. OMB's 2017 policy guidance to federal agencies, including OPM, states that agencies

---

[45] As stated previously, all incidents are covered regardless of the source.

[46] In GAO-17-254, we found that OPM's breach-response policies and procedures did not specifically address identity theft services, which could hinder informed decision-making by the agency on the appropriate services, if any, to offer affected individuals. Therefore, we recommended that OPM incorporate criteria and procedures for determining whether to offer identity theft services into the agency's policy on responding to data breaches. We also found that OPM had not adequately documented how it made its decisions about its 2015 breaches. We recommended that the agency implement procedures to help assure that significant decisions on the use of identity theft services would be appropriately documented. In September 2017, OPM implemented both recommendations.

[47] *See* Consolidated Appropriations Act, 2017, Pub. L. No. 115-31, § 633, 131 Stat. 135, 376.

[48] According to OPM staff, the contract was competed through a blanket purchase agreement bidding process. A blanket purchase agreement is a contracting vehicle that agencies are encouraged to use in order to easily access and acquire qualified providers on prenegotiated prices for services. The General Services Administration has established an identity theft services blanket purchase agreement, which includes selected identity theft service providers.

34 *United States Government Accountability Office*

should determine appropriate information to provide to affected individuals and review breach responses annually. Consistent with that guidance, OPM's September 2017 Breach Response Plan calls for the agency to review its breach response plan annually, including to reinforce or improve training and awareness. In December 2018, OPM updated its website to incorporate changes in the cost of credit freezes and duration of fraud alerts resulting from new legislation we discussed earlier.

OMB Has Not Revised Post-Data Breach Guidance to Agencies and Insurance Coverage Amount for Identity Theft Insurance Remains High

Data we assessed for this report support a 2017 recommendation we made to OMB and a matter for congressional consideration, both of which have not yet been implemented.[49] In our March 2017 report, we found that OMB policy guidance for federal agencies on how to prepare for and respond to data breaches did not address how agencies might assess the effectiveness of identity theft services relative to lower-cost alternatives.[50] For example, the guidance did not discuss whether identity theft services would be preferable to alternatives (such as fraud alerts, credit freezes, or the agency conducting its own database monitoring). We concluded that the guidance might not fully reflect the most useful and cost-effective options agencies should consider in response to a breach—contrary to OMB's risk-management and internal control guidance calling on federal leaders to improve effectiveness and efficiency. Therefore, we recommended that OMB conduct an analysis of the effectiveness of identity theft services relative to alternatives, and revise its guidance to

---

[49] See GAO-17-254.

[50] OMB Memorandum M-17-12. In this memorandum, OMB defines personally identifiable information as information that can be used to distinguish or trace an individual's identity, either alone or when combined with other information linked or linkable to a specific individual. OMB was directed to update this guidance by the October 2015 Cybersecurity Strategy and Implementation Plan for the Federal Civilian Government. See Office of Management and Budget, *Cybersecurity Strategy and Implementation Plan for the Federal Civilian Government*, M-16-04 (Washington, D.C.: Oct. 30, 2015).

Data Breaches

35

federal agencies in light of the analysis. In oral comments on a draft of the 2017 report, staff from OMB's Office of Information and Regulatory Affairs said that our draft recommendation to OMB on expanding OMB's guidance to federal agencies would benefit from greater specificity, and we revised this recommendation to provide greater clarity.

We contacted OMB several times between May 2018 and early March 2019 to update the status of this recommendation but as of March 2019, OMB had not responded with an update.[51] In our current review, we found that information on the effectiveness of various consumer options continues to be limited. We also found that some free and low-cost alternatives to free or fee-based identity theft services can prevent or more directly address new account fraud and some options consumers can take on their own have become less burdensome. Therefore, we stand by this recommendation.

In addition, as noted previously in this report, the identity theft insurance that OPM offered to affected individuals resulted in few insurance claims, and the amounts claimed have been small. These data are consistent with the findings of our 2017 report—which reported that the number and dollar amount of claims for identity theft generally were low.[52] They also reinforce our conclusion that the $5 million per-person coverage limit mandated by Congress likely was unnecessary and might impose costs without providing a meaningful corresponding benefit.

---

[51] GAO-17-254 also recommended that OMB explore options to address the risk of duplication in federal provision of identity theft services in response to data breaches, and take action if viable options were identified. In November 2018, OMB staff told us this recommendation would be updated as part of OMB's response to our request for the status of recommendations in our annual report on opportunities to reduce fragmentation, overlap, and duplication, reduce costs, and increase revenue, for the government. See GAO, *2018 Annual Report: Additional Opportunities to Reduce Fragmentation, Overlap, and Duplication and Achieve Other Financial Benefits*, GAO-18-371SP (Washington, D.C.: Apr. 26, 2018).

[52] GAO-17-254. We found identity theft insurance is limited in covering direct financial losses—that is, money that was stolen. Instead, the insurance generally reimburses consumers for out-of-pocket expenses they incur related to the process of restoring their identity and credit records. While the overall coverage limit for policies can be quite high (around one million dollars), the process of resolving identity theft typically does not require significant expenses, according to many providers with which we spoke and two consumer groups.

36   *United States Government Accountability Office*

Specifically, we noted that $5 million in coverage would increase federal costs unnecessarily, likely mislead consumers about the benefit of the product, and create unwarranted escalation of coverage amounts in the marketplace.

Therefore, we reiterate the matter for congressional consideration we made in our March 2017 report: in the event that Congress again requires an agency to provide individuals with identity theft insurance in response to a breach, it should consider permitting the agency to determine the appropriate level of that insurance.

AGENCY COMMENTS

We provided a draft of this report to CFPB, FTC, and OPM. The agencies provided technical comments, which we incorporated as appropriate.

We are sending copies of this report to the appropriate congressional committees, the Director of CFPB, the Chair of FTC, and the Acting Director of OPM.

Anna Maria Ortiz
Acting Director, Financial Markets and Community Investment

APPENDIX I: OBJECTIVES, SCOPE, AND METHODOLOGY

This report examines (1) information and expert views about the effectiveness of options consumers can use to prevent or address the risks resulting from data breaches; and (2) federal assistance available to help consumers understand these options, including the status of one matter for congressional consideration and one recommendation relating to these issues in our 2017 report.[53]

To address the first objective, we conducted a literature review to identify any studies or independent research on the effectiveness of various options consumers have for mitigating data breach harms, consumer attitudes and behavior following data breaches, and identity theft and other harm to individuals from exposure of personal information. We searched databases of scholarly publications and other sources for work generally published within the last 5 years. Examples of databases searched include ProQuest, EconLit, Policy File Index, and SciTech Premium Collection. We searched for terms including "effective," "data breach," "identity theft," "consumer attitudes," and "consumer behavior" and options such as "credit freeze," "fraud alert," and "credit lock." We also reviewed relevant academic literature to identify additional studies. From these searches, we did not identify any studies that assessed the extent to which commercial identity theft services were effective in preventing or mitigating harm from exposure of personal information. We identified and reviewed 54 studies that appeared in peer-reviewed journals or research institutions' publications and were relevant to consumer attitudes and behavior related to privacy, data breaches, and identity theft.

To ensure the selection of a range of perspectives on the effectiveness of options to mitigate harms, we reviewed the selection of experts and sources in our prior report and our literature review, and updated that selection through additional searches and recommendations from discussions with experts and identity theft service providers and review of relevant literature. We defined experts as those representing consumer and industry policy organizations that have conducted research or taken policy positions on consumers' or entities' options after data breaches; academics who conducted research on relevant topics; and federal and state government staff with specific positions of responsibility in consumer

---

[53] See GAO, Identity Theft Services: Services Offer Some Benefits but Are Limited in Preventing Fraud, GAO-17-254 (Washington, D.C.: Mar. 30, 2017).

38 *United States Government Accountability Office*

protection or education. We also contacted seven companies that provide identity theft services to consumers.

We interviewed representatives of a nongeneralizable sample of 35 entities in the following categories: academic or independent research institution (4); consumer or privacy research and advocacy (10); industry association, identity theft service provider, or industry consultant (12); and federal or state government (9). We also reviewed relevant consumer education and other materials produced by consumer, government, industry, and other entities. We interviewed academics from Carnegie-Mellon University, RAND Corporation, the University of Maryland, and the University of Rochester. In addition, we interviewed representatives from the following organizations:

- *Consumer or privacy groups:* AARP, Consumer Action, Consumer Federation of America, Consumer Reports, Electronic Privacy Information Center, Identity Theft Resource Center, National Consumer Law Center, Privacy Rights Clearinghouse, U.S. PIRG, and World Privacy Forum.
- *Industry associations or consultants:* American Bankers Association, Consumer Data Industry Association, Property and Casualty Insurers Association of America, National Retail Federation, and Rational 360.
- *Identity theft service providers:* Credit Karma, Equifax, Experian, ID Experts, ID Shield, LifeLock, and TransUnion.[54]
- *Government agencies:* Consumer Financial Protection Bureau (CFPB), Federal Reserve Bank of Philadelphia, Federal Trade Commission (FTC), Office of Personnel Management (OPM), and Offices of the Attorney General of California, Connecticut, Illinois, Massachusetts, and New York.[55]

---

[54] We also reviewed the website of Credit Sesame.

[55] We also reviewed the websites of the Offices of the Attorney General of Florida, Indiana, and Texas and of the Colorado Office of Victims Services.

Data Breaches   39

Throughout this report, we use certain qualifiers when describing responses from interview participants and views of entities whose articles and written material we reviewed, such as "few," "some," and "most." We define few as a small number such as two or three. The specific quantification of categories depends on the overall numbers of entities that addressed a specific topic. For example, we may refer to views shared by a proportion of the 10 consumer groups we interviewed, or those shared by identity theft service providers.

We also reviewed provisions in the Economic Growth, Regulatory Relief, and Consumer Protection Act, enacted in May 2018, that address credit freezes and fraud alerts (two tools for preventing new-account fraud).[56]

To address the second objective, we reviewed and analyzed documentation and interviewed staff from FTC, CFPB, and OPM. We reviewed and analyzed FTC, CFPB, and OPM consumer education materials including blog posts, online fact sheets, and printed brochures and data on usage of the materials. For example, we analyzed FTC, CFPB, and OPM data and website analytics for their data breach- and identity theft-related web pages. We interviewed FTC and CFPB agency staff about their assistance to individuals and how they measure effectiveness of their efforts. We reviewed documentation and interviewed agency staff about the development, implementation, and assessment of consumer education materials and other resources and assistance. For example, we reviewed materials documenting FTC's outreach to stakeholders and usability testing of IdentityTheft.gov.

We compared the activities against a 2014 Executive Order on the security of consumer financial transactions, key practices for consumer education planning we identified in prior work, and federal standards for internal control.[57]

---

[56] Pub. L. No. 115-174, § 301(a), 132 Stat. 1296, 1326 (2018) (codified at 15 U.S.C. § 1681c–1(i)).

[57] Exec. Order No. 13681 79 Fed. Reg. 63491(Oct. 23, 2014). See GAO, Digital Television Transition: Increased Federal Planning and Risk Management Could Further Facilitate the DTV Transition, GAO-08-43 (Washington, D.C.: Nov. 19, 2007); and Standards for Internal Control in the Federal Government, GAO-14-704G (Washington, D.C.: Sept, 10,

40 *United States Government Accountability Office*

We analyzed data from the company with which OPM contracted to provide identity theft services to the approximately 22.1 million individuals whose information was exposed in the 2015 data breaches. We obtained data on the number of enrollments, the number and size of identity theft insurance claims submitted and paid, and number of identity restoration cases the companies handled. We assessed the reliability of the data by interviewing agency officials and reviewing documentation about the systems used to store the data. We found the data to be reliable for purposes of this reporting objective. We also reviewed the online guidance OPM provided to affected individuals and assessed the guidance against Office of Management and Budget guidance for agencies following data breaches and OPM's 2017 Breach Response plan.

In addition, for both objectives, we reviewed the evidence gathered and analyzed for the 2017 GAO report (GAO-17-254) and updated the status of the matter for congressional consideration and recommendations made in that report.[58]

We conducted this performance audit from November 2017 to March 2019 in accordance with generally accepted government auditing standards. Those standards require that we plan and perform the audit to obtain sufficient, appropriate evidence to provide a reasonable basis for our findings and conclusions based on our audit objectives. We believe that the evidence obtained provides a reasonable basis for our findings and conclusions based on our audit objectives.

APPENDIX II: WHAT CAN CONSUMERS DO AFTER A DATA BREACH?

Figure 3 below provides information on actions consumers can take to monitor for identity theft or other forms of fraud, protect their personal

---

2014). Also see Office of Management and Budget, *Preparing for and Responding to a Breach of Personally Identifiable Information*, M-17-12 (Washington, D.C.: Jan. 3, 2017).

[58] See GAO, *Identity Theft Services: Services Offer Some Benefits but Are Limited in Preventing Fraud*, GAO-17-254 (Washington, D.C.: Mar. 30, 2017).

Data Breaches

41

information, and respond if they have been a victim of identity theft. This information summarizes prior GAO work and comments of academic, consumer organization, industry, and government experts.[59]

Prevent Fraud on New Credit Accounts		
Consumer Option	How This Option Can Help	Consumers Should Be Aware
Place a credit freeze on credit reports at Equifax, Experian, and TransUnion—the three nationwide consumer reporting agencies.	• Prevents identity thieves from opening new credit accounts in an individual's name—where credit reports are required. • Guardians can place credit freezes for minor children (under age 16) or adults who are incapacitated.	• Consumers must request a freeze at each of the three agencies separately. • Could still cause delays in approval of loans or other credit applications, especially if consumer forgets or loses the personal information number (PIN) the agencies give to consumers to unfreeze their credit reports. • Freezes do not prevent fraud on existing accounts (for example, the use of a stolen credit card number to make charges on a credit card). • Freezes do not prevent other types of harm, such as tax refund or medical identity fraud. • Not all access to credit reports is frozen (for example, still allowed for insurance underwriting and employment background checks). • Credit reports at agencies other than Equifax, Experian, and TransUnion will not be frozen (for example, those used to open utility accounts).
Place a fraud alert at the three nationwide consumer reporting agencies, which lasts 1 year and can be renewed.	• Fraud alerts let businesses know that a consumer may have been a victim of fraud. • Businesses must take extra steps to verify the identity of the individual seeking to open accounts. • Members of the military can place active duty alerts.	• Consumers can request a fraud alert at one of the three agencies and this agency must notify the other two to place the alert. • Victims of identity theft can place extended fraud alerts that last for 7 years. • Fraud alerts still allow access to credit reports. • Businesses that do not use the three agencies will not see the alert.

Source: GAO analysis, Federal Trade Commission, Consumer Financial Protection Bureau, and consumer and industry organizations.

Figure 3. (Continued).

---

[59] GAO, *Identity Theft Services: Services Offer Some Benefits but Are Limited in Preventing Fraud*, GAO-17-254 (Washington, D.C.: Mar. 30, 2017).

42   *United States Government Accountability Office*

Monitor for Some Types of Fraud on Financial Accounts

Consumer Option	How This Option Can Help	Consumers Should Be Aware
Review free credit reports every 12 months (from Equifax, Experian, and TransUnion) at annualcreditreport.com.	• Can help consumers spot suspicious activity or fraud involving credit accounts.	• Consumers can check one of the three reports every 4 months to improve chances of catching problems throughout the year.
Review bank and other financial account statements regularly or set up free automatic alerts.	• Can alert consumers to suspicious activity on their accounts.	• The availability and features of alerts may vary among financial institutions.
Consider enrolling in credit or identity monitoring services.	• Credit monitoring can alert consumers after the fact that someone may have used their personal information to open a credit account (take out a loan or sign up for a credit card). • Identity monitoring can alert consumers of misuse of personal information or appearance of their information on illicit websites (the "dark web").	• These services do not directly address risks of medical identity theft, identity theft tax refund fraud, or government benefits fraud. • Credit monitoring can spot fraud but generally cannot prevent it, and does not identify fraud on existing or noncredit accounts. • Identity monitoring also cannot prevent fraud. • It is unclear what actions consumers can take once alerted that their information appears on the dark web other than continuing to monitor their accounts. • These services may be part of a package of identity theft services, including restoration services, or identity theft insurance. • Free services that entities that have experienced data breaches may offer to affected consumers vary in the type and level of service and may only last for 1-2 years. Risks can exist for much longer. • Paid services typically cost $5–$30 a month.

Monitor for Other Types of Identity Theft or Fraud

Consumer Option	How This Option Can Help	Consumers Should Be Aware
Mobile Phone or Utility Account Fraud		
Review mobile phone and utility bills regularly.	• Can spot suspicious activity on existing accounts.	• Consumers with credit freezes may need to lift them before applying for new utility or phone accounts.
Medical Identity Theft		
Review medical bills and health insurance explanations of benefits.	• Can spot suspicious activity, such as bills or insurance claims for services consumers did not receive.	• Consumers who spot problems can contact fraud departments at health insurers.

Source: GAO analysis, Federal Trade Commission, Consumer Financial Protection Bureau, and consumer and industry organizations.

Figure 3. (Continued).

Data Breaches

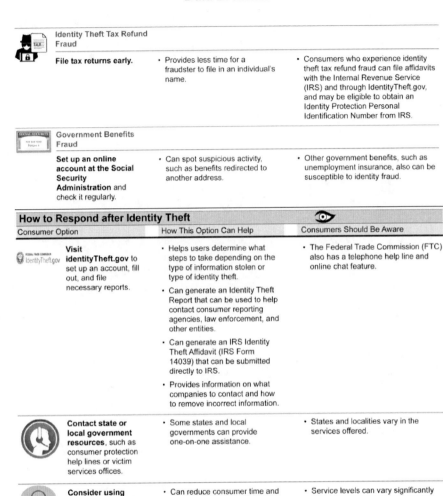

Source: GAO analysis, Federal Trade Commission, Consumer Financial Protection Bureau, and consumer and industry organizations.

Figure 3. (Continued).

44 United States Government Accountability Office

Protect Personal Information in Other Ways		
Consumer Option	How This Option Can Help	Consumers Should Be Aware
Adopt Good Practices for Online Accounts • Protect passwords and do not re-use them. • Use two-factor authentication when offered (for example, entering a one-time code sent to a mobile phone when logging in to an online account). • Choose strong passwords and consider using a software application that helps manage passwords. • Do not click on links in emails or open attachments from unknown senders. • Remember that public WiFi may not be secure.	• Can prevent unauthorized access to online accounts and other data intrusions.	• While personal security practices are important, consumers have limited control over how private entities secure their data.
Protect social media accounts by checking privacy settings, and consider limiting information shared.	• Restricts how much information is visible to strangers and their ability to misuse it.	• Privacy terms and conditions can change, so it is important to check settings periodically.
Do not provide personal information over the phone (or by email or text) unless you've initiated the call (or communication).	• Prevents identity thieves from obtaining information that can be used to commit fraud.	• Consumers can do online searches to verify identities of requesters, or check with experts, before giving out information. • Consumers should not trust caller ID and should hang up on robocalls and report such calls to FTC at ftc.gov/complaint.
Shred documents and mail with Social Security numbers or other personal information.	• Prevents identity thieves from finding sensitive information in trash.	• Consumers can contact the U.S. Postal Service if they believe their mail is being stolen or misdirected. • Consumers can opt out of receiving credit card and other offers in the mail at 1-888-5-OPT-OUT (1-888-567-8688) or www.optoutprescreen.com.

Source: GAO analysis, Federal Trade Commission, Consumer Financial Protection Bureau, and consumer and industry organizations.

Figure 3. What Can Consumers Do After a Data Breach?

In: Government Reports ...
Editor: Mathias Schweitzer

ISBN: 978-1-53615-848-9
© 2019 Nova Science Publishers, Inc.

Chapter 2

INTERNET PRIVACY AND DATA SECURITY: ADDITIONAL FEDERAL AUTHORITY COULD ENHANCE CONSUMER PROTECTION AND PROVIDE FLEXIBILITY[*]

Alicia Puente Cackley

Chairman Portman, Ranking Member Carper, and Members of the Subcommittee:

Thank you for the opportunity to testify today about Internet privacy and data security issues. The United States does not have a comprehensive data privacy law at the federal level and instead relies in part on a sectoral approach with industry-specific laws enforced by various agencies governing areas such as healthcare and financial services. In addition, the Federal Trade Commission (FTC) currently has the lead in overseeing Internet privacy across all industries, with some exceptions. Specifically, FTC addresses consumer concerns about Internet privacy using its broad

---

[*] This is an edited, reformatted and augmented accessible version of the United States Government Accountability Office Testimony Before the Permanent Subcommittee on Investigations, Committee on Homeland Security and Governmental Affairs, U.S. Senate, Publication No. GAO-19-427T, dated March 7, 2019.

authority to protect consumers from unfair and deceptive trade practices. FTC has jurisdiction over a broad range of entities and activities that are part of the Internet economy, including websites, applications (apps), advertising networks, data brokers, device manufacturers, and others.

My testimony today addresses (1) FTC's role and authorities for overseeing Internet privacy, (2) stakeholders' views on potential actions to enhance federal oversight of consumers' Internet privacy, and (3) breaches of personally identifiable information. This statement is primarily based on our January 2019 report on Internet privacy.[1] This work included evaluating FTC's Internet privacy enforcement actions and authorities and interviewing various stakeholders, including representatives from industry, consumer advocacy groups, and academia, as well as FTC staff and former FTC and Federal Communications Commission (FCC) commissioners. We also interviewed officials from other federal oversight agencies—such as the Consumer Financial Protection Bureau (CFPB), Food and Drug Administration (FDA), and the Equal Employment Opportunity Commission (EEOC)— about the strengths and limitations of their regulatory and enforcement authorities and approaches. A complete description of our scope and methodology can be found in our January 2019 report. This statement also includes some additional information on data breaches from our August 2018 report on Equifax.[2]

We conducted the performance audit on which this statement is primarily based from October 2017 through January 2019 in accordance with generally accepted government auditing standards. Those standards require that we plan and perform the audit to obtain sufficient, appropriate evidence to provide a reasonable basis for our findings and conclusions based on our audit objectives. We believe that the evidence obtained provides a reasonable basis for our findings and conclusions based on our audit objectives.

---

[1] GAO, *Internet Privacy: Additional Federal Authority Could Enhance Consumer Protection and Provide Flexibility*, GAO-19-52 (Washington, D.C.: Jan. 15, 2019).
[2] GAO, *Data Protection: Actions Taken by Equifax and Federal Agencies in Response to the 2017 Breach*, GAO-18-559 (Washington, D.C.: Aug. 30, 2018).

BACKGROUND

In April 2018, Facebook disclosed that a Cambridge University researcher may have improperly shared the data of up to 87 million of Facebook's users with a political consulting firm. This followed other incidents in recent years involving the misuse of consumers' personal information from the Internet, which about three-quarters of Americans use. These types of incidents have raised public concern because Internet-based services and products, which are essential for everyday social and economic purposes, often collect and use various forms of personal information that could cause users harm if released.

The federal privacy framework for private-sector companies is comprised of a set of tailored laws that govern the use and protection of personal information for specific purposes, in certain situations, or by certain sectors or types of entities. Such laws protect consumers' personal information related to their eligibility for credit, financial transactions, and personal health, among other areas.[3]

We reported in 2013 that no overarching federal privacy law governs the collection and sale of personal information among private-sector companies, including information resellers—companies that collect and resell information on individuals.[4] We found that gaps exist in the federal privacy framework, which does not fully address changes in technology and the marketplace. We recommended that Congress consider legislation to strengthen the consumer privacy framework to reflect the effects of changes in technology and the marketplace. Such legislation has not been enacted.

---

[3] These laws include the Fair Credit Reporting Act, the Gramm-Leach-Bliley Act, and the Health Insurance Portability and Accountability Act.

[4] GAO, *Information Resellers: Consumer Privacy Framework Needs to Reflect Changes in Technology and the Marketplace,* GAO-13-663 (Washington, D.C.: Sept. 25, 2013).

FTC's Role and Authorities for Overseeing Internet Privacy

As we reported in January 2019, FTC is primarily a law enforcement agency with authority to, among other things, address consumer concerns about Internet privacy, both for Internet service providers and content providers. It does so using its general authority under section 5 of the FTC Act, which prohibits "unfair or deceptive acts or practices in or affecting commerce."[5]

Even though the FTC Act does not speak in explicit terms about protecting consumer privacy, the Act authorizes such protection to the extent it involves practices FTC defines as unfair or deceptive. According to FTC, an act or practice is "unfair" if it causes, or is likely to cause, substantial injury not reasonably avoidable by consumers and not outweighed by countervailing benefits to consumers or competition as a result of the practice. FTC has used this "unfairness" authority to address situations where a company has allegedly failed to properly protect consumers' data, for example. According to FTC, a representation or omission is "deceptive" if it is material and is likely to mislead consumers acting reasonably under the circumstances. FTC has applied this "deceptiveness" authority to address deceptions related to violations of written privacy policies and representations concerning data security, for example.

FTC staff investigate Internet privacy complaints from various sources and also initiate investigations on their own. If FTC staff have reason to believe that an entity is engaging in an unfair or deceptive practice, they may forward an enforcement recommendation to the commission. The commission then determines whether to pursue an enforcement action.[6] With certain exceptions, FTC generally cannot directly impose civil monetary penalties for Internet privacy cases. Instead, FTC typically

---

[5] 15 U.S.C. § 45(a)(1).

[6] FTC staff operate separately from the FTC commission itself, which is the set of five commissioners, including the chair, who ultimately have responsibility for deciding upon courses of action, including enforcement actions.

Internet Privacy and Data Security

addresses Internet privacy cases by entering into settlement agreements requiring companies to take actions such as implementing reasonable privacy and security programs. If a company then violates its settlement agreement with FTC, the agency can request civil monetary penalties in court for the violations. In addition, FTC can seek to impose civil monetary penalties directly for violations of certain statutes and their implementing regulations, such as the statute pertaining to the Internet privacy of children and its corresponding regulations.

FTC has not promulgated rules under section 5 specific to Internet privacy. According to FTC staff, the process the agency must use to issue such rules—known as the Magnuson-Moss procedures—includes steps that add time and complexity to the rulemaking process. FTC has not promulgated any regulations using the Magnuson-Moss procedures since 1980. Although FTC has not implemented its section 5 authority by issuing regulations regarding internet privacy, it has issued regulations when directed and authorized by Congress to implement other statutory authorities using a different set of rulemaking procedures. These procedures, spelled out in section 553 of the Administrative Procedures Act (APA),[7] are those that most federal agencies typically use to develop and issue regulations.

APA section 553 establishes procedures and requirements for what is known as "informal" rulemaking, also known as notice-and-comment rulemaking. Among other things, section 553 generally requires agencies to publish a notice of proposed rulemaking in the Federal Register. After giving interested persons an opportunity to comment on the proposal by providing "data, views, or arguments," the statute then requires the agency to publish the final rule in the Federal Register.

In contrast, the rulemaking procedures that FTC generally must follow to issue rules under the FTC Act are the Magnuson-Moss procedures noted above. These are required by the Magnuson-Moss Warranty Act amendments to the FTC Act and impose additional rulemaking steps beyond APA section 553. These steps include providing the public and

---

[7] 5 U.S.C. § 553.

certain congressional committees with an advance notice of proposed rulemaking (in addition to the notice of proposed rulemaking). FTC's rulemaking under Magnuson-Moss also calls for, among other things, oral hearings, if requested, presided over by an independent hearing officer and preparation of a staff report after the conclusion of public hearings, giving the public the opportunity to comment on the report.

FTC has promulgated regulations using the APA section 553 notice-and comment rulemaking procedures when authorized or directed by specific statutes. For example, the 1998 Children's Online Privacy Protection Act (COPPA) required FTC to issue regulations concerning children's online privacy; promulgate these regulations using the APA section 553 process; and, in determining how to treat a violation of the rules, to treat it as an unfair or deceptive act or practice in most cases. COPPA governs the online collection of personal information from children under the age of 13 by operators of websites or online services, including mobile applications. COPPA contained a number of specific requirements that FTC was directed to implement by regulation, such as requiring websites to post a complete privacy policy, to notify parents directly about their information collection practices, and to obtain verifiable parental consent before collecting personal information from their children or sharing it with others.

Laws and regulations may be enforced in various ways, for example, by seeking civil monetary penalties for non-compliance. As mentioned, FTC has authority to seek civil monetary penalties when a company violates a settlement agreement or certain statutes or regulations. For example, in March 2018, FTC announced that it is investigating whether Facebook's current privacy practices violate a settlement agreement that the company entered into with FTC. In the case that resulted in the 2012 settlement, FTC had charged Facebook with deceiving consumers by telling them they could keep their information private, but then allowing it to be shared and made public. FTC also has authority to seek civil monetary penalties for violations of the COPPA statute as well as FTC's COPPA regulations.

In our January 2019 Internet privacy report, we found that during the last decade, FTC filed 101 Internet privacy enforcement actions to address practices that the agency alleged were unfair, deceptive, a violation of COPPA, a violation of a settlement agreement, or a combination of those reasons. Most of these actions pertained to first-time violations of the FTC Act for which FTC does not have authority to levy civil monetary penalties. In nearly all 101 cases, companies settled with FTC, which required the companies to make changes in their policies or practices as part of the settlement.

STAKEHOLDERS AND FTC IDENTIFIED POTENTIAL ACTIONS TO ENHANCE FEDERAL OVERSIGHT OF CONSUMERS' INTERNET PRIVACY

Various stakeholders we interviewed for our January 2019 Internet privacy report said that opportunities exist for enhancing Internet privacy oversight. Most industry stakeholders said they favored FTC's current approach—direct enforcement of its unfair and deceptive practices statutory authority, rather than promulgating and enforcing regulations implementing that authority. These stakeholders said that the current approach allows for flexibility; that regulations could hinder innovation, create loopholes, and become obsolete; and that rulemakings can be lengthy. Other stakeholders, including consumer advocates and most former FTC and FCC commissioners we interviewed, favored having FTC issue and enforce regulations. Stakeholders said that regulations can provide clarity, flexibility, and act as a deterrent, and may also promote fairness by giving companies notice of what actions are prohibited.

Those stakeholders who believe that FTC's current authority and enforcement approach is unduly limited identified three main actions that could better protect Internet privacy: (1) enactment of an overarching federal privacy statute to establish general requirements governing Internet privacy practices of all sectors, (2) APA section 553 notice-andcomment

52   *Alicia Puente Cackley*

rulemaking authority, and (3) civil penalty authority for any violation of a statutory or regulatory requirement, rather than allowing penalties only for violations of settlement agreements or consent decrees that themselves seek redress for a previous statutory or regulatory violation.

Privacy Statute

Stakeholders from a variety of perspectives—including academia, industry, consumer advocacy groups, and former FTC and FCC commissioners—told us that a statute could enhance Internet privacy oversight by, for example, clearly articulating to consumers, industry, and privacy enforcers what behaviors are prohibited. Some stakeholders suggested that such a framework could either designate an existing agency (such as FTC) as responsible for privacy oversight or create a new agency. For example, in Canada, the Office of the Privacy Commissioner, an independent body that reports directly to the Parliament, was established to protect and promote individuals' privacy rights.

Some stakeholders also stated that the absence of a comprehensive Internet privacy statute affects FTC's enforcement. For example, a former federal enforcement official from another oversight agency said that FTC is limited in how it can use its authority to take action against companies' unfair and deceptive trade practices for problematic Internet privacy practices. Similarly, another former federal enforcement official from another agency said that FTC is limited in how and against whom it can use its unfair and deceptive practices authority noting, for example, that it cannot pursue Internet privacy enforcement against exempted industries.[8]

In addition, some stakeholders said FTC's section 5 unfair and deceptive practices authority may not enable it to fully protect consumers' Internet privacy because it can be difficult for FTC to establish that Internet privacy practices are legally unfair. Because of this difficulty,

---

[8] The FTC Act prohibits FTC from taking action against companies such as telecommunications carriers, airlines and railroads under certain circumstances. FTC also does not have jurisdiction over banks, credit unions, or savings and loans institutions.

Internet Privacy and Data Security

some stakeholders said that FTC relies more heavily on its authority to take enforcement action against deceptive trade practices compared with the agency's unfair trade practices authority. This is consistent with the results of our analysis of FTC cases, which showed that in a majority of the actions FTC settled, FTC alleged that companies engaged in practices that were deceptive. Furthermore, a recently decided federal appeals court case illustrates potential limits on FTC's enforcement remedies. The court found that FTC could not direct the company, which was accused of unfair practices, to create and implement comprehensive data security measures for the personal information the company stored on its computer networks as a remedy for the practices alleged. Instead, the court ruled that FTC's authority was limited to prohibiting specific illegal practices.[9]

APA Notice-and-Comment Rulemaking

Various stakeholders said that there are advantages to overseeing Internet privacy with a statute that provides APA section 553 notice-and-comment rulemaking authority. Officials from other consumer and worker protection agencies we interviewed described their enforcement authorities and approaches. For example, officials from CFPB and FDA, both of which use APA section 553 notice-and-comment rulemaking, said that their rulemaking authority assists in their oversight approaches and supports their enforcement actions. EEOC officials said that regulations are used to guide investigations that establish whether enforcement action is appropriate.

---

[9] In this case, FTC filed a complaint against LabMD, a medical laboratory, under section 5 of the FTC Act for allegedly committing an unfair act or practice by failing to provide reasonable and appropriate security for personal information on its computer networks. On appeal, the Eleventh Circuit ruled that FTC's cease and desist order exceeded its authority because it did not prohibit a specific act or practice but instead, mandated a complete overhaul of the company's data-security program. *LabMD, Inc. v. FTC*, 891 F.3d 1286 (11th Cir. 2018).

Ability to Levy Civil Penalties for Initial Violations

Some stakeholders suggested that FTC's ability to levy civil penalties could also be enhanced. As noted, FTC can levy civil penalties against companies for violating certain regulations, such as COPPA regulations, or for violating the terms of a settlement agreement already in place. According to most former FTC commissioners and some other stakeholders we interviewed, FTC should be able to levy fines for initial violations of section 5 of the FTC Act. An academic told us that the power of an agency to levy a fine is a tangible way to hold industries accountable.

BREACHES INVOLVING PERSONALLY IDENTIFIABLE INFORMATION HIGHLIGHT THE IMPORTANCE OF SECURITY AND PRIVACY

Recent data breaches at federal agencies, retailers, hospitals, insurance companies, consumer reporting agencies, and other large organizations highlight the importance of ensuring the security and privacy of personally identifiable information collected and maintained by those entities. Such breaches have resulted in the potential compromise of millions of Americans' personally identifiable information, which could lead to identity theft and other serious consequences. For example, the breach of an Equifax online dispute portal from May to July 2017 resulted in the compromise of records containing the personally identifiable information of at least 145.5 million consumers in the United States and nearly 1 million consumers outside the United States. We reported in August 2018 that Equifax's investigation of the breach identified four major factors—identification, detection, segmenting of access to databases, and data governance—that allowed the attacker to gain access to its network and extract information from databases containing personally identifiable

Internet Privacy and Data Security 55

information.[10] In September 2017, FTC and CFPB, which both have regulatory and enforcement authority over consumer reporting agencies such as Equifax, initiated an investigation into the breach and Equifax's response. Their investigation is ongoing.

According to a 2017 National Telecommunications and Information Administration (NTIA) survey conducted by the U.S. Census Bureau, 24 percent of American households surveyed avoided making financial transactions on the Internet due to privacy or security concerns.[11] NTIA's survey results show that privacy concerns may lead to lower levels of economic productivity if people decline to make financial transactions on the Internet. Consumers who were surveyed indicated that their specific concerns were identity theft, credit card or banking fraud, data collection by online services, loss of control over personal information, data collection by government, and threats to personal safety.

Recent data breaches and developments regarding Internet privacy suggest that this is an appropriate time for Congress to consider what additional actions are needed to protect consumer privacy, including comprehensive Internet privacy legislation. Although FTC has been addressing Internet privacy through its unfair and deceptive practices authority and FTC and other agencies have been addressing this issue using statutes that target specific industries or consumer segments, the lack of a comprehensive federal privacy statute leaves consumers' privacy at risk. Comprehensive legislation addressing Internet privacy that establishes specific standards and includes APA notice-and-comment rulemaking and first-time violation civil penalty authorities could enhance the federal government's ability to protect consumer privacy, provide more certainty in the marketplace as companies innovate and develop new products using consumer data, and provide better assurance to consumers that their privacy will be protected. In our January 2019 report, we recommended that Congress consider developing comprehensive legislation on Internet

---

[10] GAO-18-559.

[11] NTIA, *Most Americans Continue to Have Privacy and Security Concerns, NTIA Survey Finds* (Washington, D.C.: Aug. 20, 2018) *available at* https://www.ntia.doc.gov/blog/2018/most-americans-continue-have-privacy-and-securityconcerns-ntia-survey-finds (last visited Mar. 5, 2019).

privacy that would enhance consumer protections and provide flexibility to address a rapidly evolving Internet environment. Issues that should be considered include:

- which agency or agencies should oversee Internet privacy;
- what authorities an agency or agencies should have to oversee Internet privacy, including notice-and-comment rulemaking authority and first-time violation civil penalty authority; and
- how to balance consumers' need for Internet privacy with industry's ability to provide services and innovate.

Chairman Portman, Ranking Member Carper, and Members of the Subcommittee, this concludes my prepared statement. I would be pleased to respond to any questions you may have at this time.

In: Government Reports …
Editor: Mathias Schweitzer

ISBN: 978-1-53615-848-9
© 2019 Nova Science Publishers, Inc.

Chapter 3

DOD SPACE ACQUISITIONS: INCLUDING USERS EARLY AND OFTEN IN SOFTWARE DEVELOPMENT COULD BENEFIT PROGRAMS[*]

United States Government Accountability Office

ABBREVIATIONS

ACAT	Acquisition Category
DevOps	Development and Operations
DDS	Defense Digital Service
DOD	Department of Defense
DODI	Department of Defense Instruction
DSB	Defense Science Board
FAB-T	Family of Advanced Beyond

---

[*] This is an edited, reformatted and augmented version of United States Government Accountability Office; Report to Congressional Committees; Accessible Version, Publication No. GAO-19-136, dated March 2019.

	Line-of-Sight Terminals
FITARA	Federal Information Technology Acquisition Reform Act
FFRDC	Federally Funded Research and Development Center
GPS	Global Positioning System
IEC	International Electrotechnical Commission
IEEE	Institute of Electrical and Electronics Engineers
ISO	International Organization for Standardization
IT	Information Technology
JMS Inc. 2	Joint Space Operations Center Mission System Increment 2
JSpOC	Joint Space Operations Center
MAIS	Major Acquisition Information System
MDAP	Major Defense Acquisition Program
MUOS	Mobile User Objective System
NDAA	National Defense Authorization Act
OCX	Next Generation Operational Control System
SBIRS	Space-Based Infrared System
SMDC/ ARSTRAT	Space and Missile Defense Command/Army Forces Strategic Command
USSTRATCOM	U.S. Strategic Command

WHY GAO DID THIS STUDY

Over the next 5 years, DOD plans to spend over $65 billion on its space system acquisitions portfolio, including many systems that rely on software for key capabilities. However, software-intensive space systems have had a history of significant schedule delays and billions of dollars in cost growth.

Senate and House reports accompanying the National Defense Authorization Act for Fiscal Year 2017 contained provisions for GAO to review challenges in software-intensive DOD space programs. This report addresses, among other things, (1) the extent to which these programs have involved users; and (2) what software-specific management challenges, if any, programs faced.

To do this work, GAO reviewed four major space defense programs with cost growth or schedule delays caused, in part, by software. GAO reviewed applicable statutes and DOD policies and guidance that identified four characteristics of effective user engagement. GAO reviewed program documentation; and interviewed program officials, contractors, and space systems users. GAO also analyzed program metrics, test and evaluation reports, and external program assessments.

WHAT GAO RECOMMENDS

GAO is making two recommendations that DOD ensure its guidance that addresses software development provides specific, required direction on the timing, frequency, and documentation of user involvement and feedback. DOD concurred with the recommendations.

WHAT GAO FOUND

The four major Department of Defense (DOD) software-intensive space programs that GAO reviewed struggled to effectively engage system users. These programs are the Air Force's Joint Space Operations Center Mission System Increment 2 (JMS), Next Generation Operational Control System (OCX), Space-Based Infrared System (SBIRS); and the Navy's Mobile User Objective System (MUOS). These ongoing programs are estimated to cost billions of dollars, have experienced overruns of up to three times originally estimated cost, and have been in development for periods ranging from 5 to over 20 years. Previous GAO reports, as well as DOD and industry studies, have found that user involvement is critical to

60 *United States Government Accountability Office*

the success of any software development effort. For example, GAO previously reported that obtaining frequent feedback is linked to reducing risk, improving customer commitment, and improving technical staff motivation. However, the programs GAO reviewed often did not demonstrate characteristics of effective user engagement that are identified in DOD policy and statute:

- Early engagement. OCX involved users early; JMS planned to but, in practice, did not; SBIRS and MUOS did not plan to involve users early.
- Continual engagement. JMS, OCX, and SBIRS all planned to continually involve users but, in practice, did not fully do so; MUOS did not plan to do so.
- Feedback based on actual working software. OCX and SBIRS provided users opportunities to give such feedback but only years into software development; JMS and MUOS did not provide opportunities for feedback.
- Feedback incorporated into subsequent development. JMS, OCX, and SBIRS all planned to incorporate user feedback but, in practice, have not done so throughout development; MUOS did not plan to do so.

As reflected above, actual program efforts to involve users and obtain and incorporate feedback were often unsuccessful. This was due, in part, to the lack of specific guidance on user involvement and feedback. Although DOD policies state that users should be involved and provide feedback on software development projects, they do not provide specific guidance on the timing, frequency, and documentation of such efforts. Without obtaining user feedback and acceptance, programs risk delivering systems that do not meet users' needs. In selected instances, the lack of user involvement has contributed to systems that were later found to be operationally unsuitable.

The programs GAO reviewed also faced software-specific challenges in using commercial software, applying outdated software tools, and having limited knowledge and training in newer software development techniques. For example, programs using commercial software often underestimated the effort required to integrate such software into an overall system. Secondly, selected programs relied on obsolete software tools that they were accustomed to using but which industry had since replaced. Finally, GAO found that two of the reviewed programs lacked knowledge of more modern software development approaches. DOD has acknowledged these challenges and has efforts underway to address each of them.

March 18, 2019
Congressional Committees

Department of Defense (DOD) space systems have grown increasingly dependent on software to enable a wide range of functions, including satellite command and control, early detection and tracking of objects in the earth's orbit, global positioning system (GPS) signals, and radio communication for military forces. Over the next 5 years, DOD plans to spend over $65 billion on its space system acquisitions portfolio, including many systems that rely on software for key capabilities. However, over the last two decades, DOD has had trouble with space acquisition programs where software is a key component, as evidenced by significant schedule delays and billions of dollars of cost growth attributable in part to software problems.

For over 30 years, we have reported on DOD's challenges in acquiring software-intensive weapon systems, including space systems.[1] These challenges include: ineffective management of system requirements, critical software design deficiencies, deferred resolution of problems to later phases of development, inadequate testing of systems, and a lack of

---

[1] For the purposes of this report, we use the international standard for software-intensive systems: any system where software contributes essential influences to the design, construction, deployment, and evolution of the system as a whole. International Organization for Standardization/International Electrotechnical Commission / Institute of Electrical and Electronics Engineers (ISO/IEC/IEEE), *International Standard, Systems and software engineering—Architecture description,* 42010 (December 2011).

62   *United States Government Accountability Office*

meaningful metrics.[2] Congress has mandated DOD to improve its approaches for software development within major defense acquisitions. For example, in 2002, Congress required that each military department establish a program to (1) improve the software acquisition process that includes efforts to develop appropriate metrics for performance measurement and continual process improvement; and (2) ensure that key program personnel have an appropriate level of experience or training in software acquisition. In 2010, Congress required that DOD implement processes to include early and continual user involvement, among other things.[3] In 2014, Congress enacted information technology (IT) acquisition reform legislation (referred to as the Federal Information Technology Acquisition Reform Act, or FITARA), which, among other things, requires covered agencies' chief information officers to certify that incremental development is adequately implemented for IT investments.[4]

---

[2] GAO, *Weapon Systems Annual Assessment: Knowledge Gaps Pose Risks to Sustaining Recent Positive Trends*, GAO-18-360SP (Washington, D.C.: Apr. 25, 2018); *Defense Acquisitions: Stronger Management Practices Are Needed to Improve DOD's Software-Intensive Weapon Acquisitions*, GAO-04-393 (Washington, D.C.: Mar. 1, 2004); *Mission-Critical Systems: Defense Attempting to Address Major Software Challenges*, GAO-93-13 (Washington, D.C.: Dec. 24, 1992); and *Space Defense: Management and Technical Problems Delay Operations Center Acquisition*, GAO/IMTEC-89-18 (Washington, D.C.: Apr. 20, 1989). For more on our previous work in this area, see the related GAO Products page at the end of this report.

[3] DOD has been directed to improve software acquisition in general and improve user involvement. In particular, the Bob Stump National Defense Authorization Act (NDAA) for Fiscal Year 2003, Pub. L. No. 107-314, § 804 (2002) requires DOD to improve the software-related weapon system acquisition processes with, at a minimum, a documented process for software acquisition planning, requirements development and management, project management and oversight, and risk management; efforts to develop appropriate metrics for performance measurement and continual process improvement; and a process to ensure that key program personnel have an appropriate level of experience or training. In addition, the Fiscal Year 2010 NDAA, Pub. L. No. 111-84, § 804 (2009) requires DOD to implement weapon system acquisition processes that are designed to include early and continual involvement of the user; multiple, rapidly executed increments or releases of capability; early, successive prototyping to support an evolutionary approach; and a modular, open-systems approach.

[4] Carl Levin and Howard P. "Buck" McKeon National Defense Authorization Act for Fiscal Year 2015, Pub. L. No. 113-291, § 831 (codified as amended at 40 U.S.C. § 11319). 40 U.S.C. § 11319(b)(1)(B)(ii) requires that, for covered agencies including DOD, the chief information officers certify that IT investments are adequately implementing incremental development, as defined in capital planning guidance issued by the Office of Management and Budget (OMB). OMB's memorandum M-15-14, Management and Oversight of Federal Information Technology (2015) defines information technology for the purposes of implementing FITARA and sets the standard for adequate incremental development of

DOD Space Acquisitions

63

In response, DOD has made efforts to improve its software development within weapon system acquisitions, such as revising the Department of Defense Instruction (DODI) 5000.02—its instruction for the management of all DOD acquisition programs—in 2015 for programs to use development approaches such as incremental development and to involve users more frequently. In addition, the DODI 5000.02 allows programs to tailor its acquisition procedures to more efficiently achieve program objectives.

Senate and House reports accompanying the National Defense Authorization Act (NDAA) for Fiscal Year 2017 contain provisions for us to review software-intensive DOD space system acquisition programs, among other things. This report addresses, for selected software-intensive space programs, (1) the extent to which these programs have involved users and delivered software using newer development approaches; and (2) what software-specific management challenges, if any, these programs have faced.

We reviewed four software-intensive major defense programs with cost growth or schedule delays attributed, in part, to software development challenges.[5] In selecting these systems from an initial list of 49 DOD space programs, we narrowed our selection to software-intensive Major Defense Acquisition Programs and Major Automated Information Systems as identified by DOD where software development has contributed in some part to cost growth or schedule delays. We further narrowed to those programs that experienced unit cost or schedule breaches or changes and

---

software or services as delivery of new or modified technical functionality to users at least every 6 months.

[5] The term "Major Defense Acquisition Program" (MDAP) means a Department of Defense acquisition program that is not a highly sensitive classified program (as determined by the Secretary of Defense) and—(1) that is designated by the Secretary of Defense as a major defense acquisition program; or (2) that is estimated by the Secretary of Defense to require an eventual total expenditure for research, development, test, and evaluation of more than $480,000,000 (based on fiscal year 2014 constant dollars) or an eventual total expenditure for procurement of more than $2,790,000,000 (based on fiscal year 2014 constant dollars). 10 U.S.C. § 2430(a); amounts and base fiscal year adjusted on the basis of Department of Defense escalation rates per 10 U.S.C. § 2430(b). Department of Defense Instruction 5000.02, Operation of the Defense Acquisition System (Enclosure 1, Acquisition Program Categories and Compliance Requirements) (Aug. 31, 2018).

64 *United States Government Accountability Office*

represented different DOD services and acquisition categories.[6] These programs are the Air Force's Joint Space Operations Center Mission System Increment 2 (JMS), Next Generation Operational Control System (OCX), Space-Based Infrared System (SBIRS); and the Navy's Mobile User Objective System (MUOS).[7]

To address the objectives, we interviewed officials from the Undersecretary of Defense for Acquisition and Sustainment, Office of the Deputy Assistant Secretary of Defense for Systems Engineering, Office of Cost Assessment and Program Evaluation, Office of the Director of Operational Test and Evaluation, Defense Digital Service, Defense Innovation Board, and the Office of the Assistant Secretary of the Air Force for Space Acquisition.[8] We also interviewed officials from the selected program offices and their respective contractors, space systems users, DOD test organizations, and Federally Funded Research and Development Centers.[9]

To determine how effectively selected DOD software-intensive space programs have involved users and adopted newer software development approaches, we reviewed the Fiscal Year 2010 NDAA, in addition to DOD's 2010 report to Congress in response to this statute, and DODI 5000.02, which identified characteristics of user engagement. We then

---

[6] The MDAP definitions for significant and critical unit cost breaches are based on unit cost growth as defined in 10 U.S.C. 2433. The Major Automated Information System (MAIS) program definitions for significant and critical changes are based on schedule, cost, or expected performance of the program were defined in 10 U.S.C. 2445c prior to repeal by the National Defense Authorization Act for Fiscal Year 2010, Pub.L. No. 111-84, § 846 (2009).

[7] We initially selected the Family of Advanced Beyond Line-of-Sight Terminals (FAB-T) program but were unable to assess the program's software issues with the same level of detail as the other programs we reviewed because, despite prior software challenges, the program stated it does not have documentation that separately tracks software-related requirements or efforts.

[8] In 2018, the Office of the Under Secretary of Defense for Acquisition and Sustainment appointed a Special Assistant for Software Acquisition to provide strategic focus and overall policy guidance on all matters of defense software acquisition. In 2015, DOD established the Defense Digital Service (DDS) to influence the way DOD builds and deploys technology and digital services. In 2016, DOD established the Defense Innovation Board to provide independent advice and recommendations on innovative ways to address future challenges in terms of integrated change to technology applications, among other things.

[9] For DOD space systems, users include operators of the system as well as end users of the data produced by the system.

reviewed relevant program plans and documentation—such as human engineering and human systems integration plans, and standard operating procedures—and interviewed program officials and end users to determine the extent to which the program addressed the characteristics. We also examined DOD guidance and applicable leading practices to identify time frames for delivering software under incremental and iterative software development approaches, and we compared these time frames to program performance.

To determine what software-specific management challenges, if any, these selected programs have faced, we reviewed GAO reports and industry reports and studies on software tools and metrics used to manage software programs and also reviewed program management reports, contract documents, and external reports. We also interviewed program and contractor officials and officials from Federally Funded Research and Development Centers. We also reviewed program metrics, test and evaluation reports, and external program assessments. See Appendix I for additional information on our objectives, scope, and methodology.

We conducted this performance audit from November 2017 to March 2019 in accordance with generally accepted government auditing standards. Those standards require that we plan and perform the audit to obtain sufficient, appropriate evidence to provide a reasonable basis for our findings and conclusions based on our audit objectives. We believe that the evidence obtained provides a reasonable basis for our findings and conclusions based on our audit objectives.

BACKGROUND

Software development approaches have evolved over time. DOD weapon system acquisition programs have traditionally developed software using what is known as the waterfall development approach, first conceived in 1970 as linear and sequential phases of development over several years that result in a single delivery of capability.[10] Figure 1 depicts an overview of the waterfall approach.

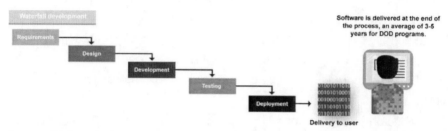

Source: GAO analysis of Department of Defense (DOD) and industry documentation. | GAO-19-136.

Figure 1. Waterfall Software Development.

Within industry, software development has evolved with the adoption of newer approaches and tools. For example, while a traditional waterfall approach usually is often broadly scoped, multiyear, and produces a product at the end of a sequence of phases, an incremental approach delivers software in smaller parts, or increments, in order to deliver capabilities more quickly. This development technique has been preferred for acquiring major federal IT systems, to the maximum extent practicable, and in OMB guidance since at least 2000.[11] In addition, iterative development promotes continual user engagement with more frequent software releases to users. Figure 2 shows an overview of incremental and iterative development.

---

[10] A 1970 paper entitled *Managing the Development of Large Software Systems,* by Dr. Winston W. Royce, is considered by the Software Engineering Institute and others to be the basis for waterfall methodology. See Royce, Winston. Managing the Development of Large Software Systems. Reprinted from *Proceedings,* IEEE WESCOM (August 1970), pages 1-9. Although the paper never uses the term "waterfall," the model has sequential phases that flow continuously from one step to the next. While the paper noted that this model is risky because it is unknown how the system will actually work until the testing phase, and recommended iterative interaction between steps, it became the foundation for what is known as the waterfall approach. In 1985, DOD released DOD Standard 2167, which required software development programs to follow a uniform process that mirrored the waterfall methodology.

[11] See Clinger-Cohen Act of 1996, Pub. L. No. 104-106, § 5202 (1996), codified at 41 U.S.C. § 2308 (agencies should use modular contracting, to the maximum extent practicable, to acquire major systems of information technology); see also FAR § 39.103; OMB, Circular No. A-130, Management of Federal Information Resources (Nov. 28, 2000).

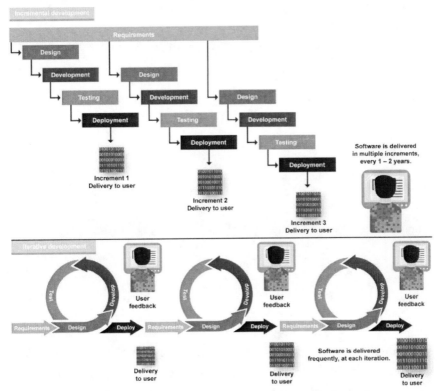

Source: GAO analysis of Department of Defense (DOD) and industry documentation. | GAO-19-136.

Figure 2. Incremental and Iterative Software Development.

DevOps is a more recent type of software development first used by industry around 2009. According to the Defense Innovation Board, DevOps represents the integration of software development and software operations, along with the tools and culture that support rapid prototyping and deployment, early engagement with the end user, and automation and monitoring of software.[12] Figure 3 shows a notional representation of the DevOps approach based on DOD and industry information. There are also a variety of other software development approaches.[13]

---

[12] Defense Innovation Board, *Ten Commandments of Software* (Apr. 20, 2018).

[13] Other approaches include Spiral Model, Lean, and others. For the purposes of this report, we focus on the newer approaches that have been adopted by the DOD software-intensive space programs in our review.

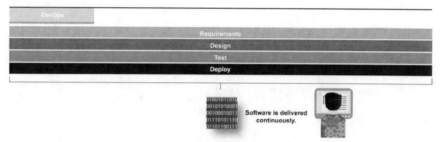

Source: GAO analysis of Department of Defense (DOD) and industry documentation. | GAO-19-136.

Figure 3. DevOps Software Development.

Incremental, Iterative, and DevOps approaches are further described as follows:

- Incremental development sets high level requirements early in the effort, and functionality is delivered in stages. Multiple increments deliver a part of the overall required program capability. Several builds and deployments are typically necessary to satisfy approved requirements. DOD guidance for incremental development for software-intensive programs states that each increment should be delivered within 2 years, and OMB guidance issued pursuant to FITARA requires delivery of software for information technology investments in 6-month increments.[14]

- Iterative development takes a flexible approach to requirements setting. In this approach, requirements are refined in iterations based on user feedback. We include Agile development approaches in this category of development; although most Agile approaches include aspects of both iterative and incremental

---

[14] DODI 5000.02 states that Incrementally Deployed Software Intensive Systems software deploys full capability in multiple increments as new capability is developed and delivered, nominally in 1-to 2-year cycles. DODI 5000.02, § 5(c)(3)(d) (Aug. 31, 2018). Pursuant to FITARA, the Office of Management and Budget guidance on information technology investments has described adequate incremental development for software as delivery of new or modified technical functionality to users at least every 6 months. For the purposes of this report, we used the upper end of the DOD range (2 years) in evaluating DOD incremental software deliveries.

development, as shown in figure 4. The Agile approach was first articulated in 2001 in what is known as the Agile Manifesto. The Agile Manifesto states the importance of four values: (1) individuals and interactions over processes and tools, (2) working software over comprehensive documentation, (3) customer collaboration over contract negotiation, and (4) responding to change as opposed to following a pre-set plan. Approaches that share common Agile principles include: Scrum, Extreme Programming, and Scaled Agile Framework, among others.[15]

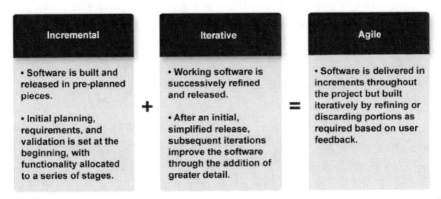

Source: GAO analysis of Department of Defense (DOD) and industry documentation. | GAO-19-136.

Figure 4. Incremental and Iterative Aspects of Agile Development.

These approaches stress delivering the most value as early as possible and constantly improving it throughout the project lifecycle based on user feedback.[16] Within industry, Agile development approaches typically complete iterations within 6 weeks, and deliver working software to the user at the end of each iteration.[17] According to DOD and industry,

---

[15] Some other key differentiators of Agile software development include: focus on consistent work velocity, focus on high software quality, and focus on maximum defect containment. For more on Agile software development, see http://agilemanifesto.org/.

[16] This initial delivery is often called a minimum viable product. Within DOD, it may be known as a minimum deployable or minimum releasable product.

[17] The National Defense Industrial Association, International Standards Organization, and other industry studies recommend deliveries of working software within a range of 1 to 6 weeks. The DOD Instruction 5000.02 (Aug. 31, 2018) does not contain guidance for iterative

70   *United States Government Accountability Office*

iterative development approaches have led to quicker development at lower costs and have provided strategic benefit through rapid response to changing user needs.[18]

- DevOps is a variation of Agile that combines "development" and "operations," emphasizing communication, collaboration, and continuous integration between both software developers and users.[19] According to the Software Engineering Institute, DevOps is commonly seen as an extension of Agile into the operations side of the process, implementing continuous delivery through automated pipelines. In general, all stakeholders—including operations staff, testers, developers, and users—are embedded on the same team from the project's inception to its end, ensuring constant communication.[20] Automated deployment and testing is used instead of a manual approach, and the developer's working copies of software are synchronized with the users. Software code is continuously integrated and delivered into production or a production-like environment. According to industry reports, the use of DevOps may lower costs due to immediate detection of problems as well as result in a greater confidence in the software because the users have continuous visibility into development, testing, and deployment.[21]

---

deliveries. For the purposes of this report, we used the upper end of the industry range (6 weeks) in evaluating DOD iterative software deliveries.

[18] Defense Science Board, *Design and Acquisition of Software for Defense Systems* (Washington D.C.: February 2018); Defense Innovation Board, *Ten Commandments of Software* (Apr. 20, 2018); National Defense Industrial Association, *An Industry Practice Guide for Agile on Earned Value Management Programs* (Arlington: Mar. 31, 2017); IBM, *Transitioning from Waterfall to Iterative Development* (Apr. 16, 2004, accessed Dec. 7, 2017), http://www.ibm.com/developerworks/rational/library/4243.html.

[19] There are multiple ways to define DevOps. For the purposes of this report, we used descriptions from DOD, Software Engineering Institute, U.S. General Services Administration, and The MITRE Corporation.

[20] Software Engineering Institute, Software and Cyber Solutions Symposium 2018: DevOps Process & Implementation for Managers and Executives (Mar. 26-28, 2018).

[21] ISO/IEC JTC1/SC7, *DevOps & Agile Study Group Report, Version 1.0,* (May 2017 to April 2018); MITRE, *DevOps for Federal Acquisition,* (2015-2018).

DOD Space Acquisitions 71

According to DOD officials from the Undersecretary of Defense, Research and Engineering, adopting Agile and DevOps within DOD weapon system acquisitions—which includes DOD space programs—is challenging and requires programs to adopt comprehensive strategies that cover broad topics. Officials said these strategies should include plans for cultural adoption by the program office and contractor; training and certification for program office and contractor personnel; and tools, metrics, and processes that support continuous integration and delivery, among others.

Collaboration between Developers and Users Is Key to Reducing Program Risk

While there are a variety of approaches to developing software, involving users in early stages and throughout software development helps detect deficiencies early. Industry studies have shown it becomes more expensive to remove conceptual flaws the later they are found.[22] Previous GAO reports as well as other DOD and industry studies have also found that user involvement is critical to the success of any software development effort.[23] For example, we previously reported that obtaining

---

[22] Software Engineering Institute, *Results of SEI Independent Research and Development Projects and Report on Emerging Technologies and Technology Trends*—Technical Report CMU/SEI-2004-TR-018, (Pittsburgh: Oct. 2004); Iosif Alvertis and Sotiris Koussouris, et al, "User Involvement in Software Development Processes," *Procedia Computer Science*, vol. 97 (2016): 73-83; JC Westland, "The Cost Of Errors In Software Development: Evidence from Industry," *The Journal of Systems and Software 62*, (2002) p.1-9; and Deloitte, *Agile in Government* (2017).

[23] GAO, *Information Technology Reform: Agencies Need to Improve Certification of Incremental Development*, GAO-18-148 (Washington, D.C.: Nov. 7, 2018); *Immigration Benefits System: U.S. Citizenship Immigration Services Can Improve Program Management*, GAO-16-467 (Washington, D.C.: July 7, 2016); *Software Development: Effective Practices and Federal Challenges in Applying Agile Methods*, GAO-12-681 (Washington, D.C.: July 27, 2012); and *Information Technology: Critical Factors Underlying Successful Major Acquisitions*, GAO-12-7 (Washington, D.C.: Oct. 21, 2011). Department of Defense, Office of the Under Secretary of Defense for Research and Engineering; Defense Science Board, *Design and Acquisition of Software for Defense Systems* (Washington D.C.: February 2018); and Software Engineering Institute, *Scaling Agile Methods for Department of Defense Programs*, Technical Note CMU/SEI-2016-TN005 (December 2016).

72   *United States Government Accountability Office*

frequent feedback is linked to reducing risk, improving customer commitment, and improving technical staff motivation.[24] We also previously reported that two factors critical to success in incremental development were involving users early in the development of requirements and prior to formal end-user testing.[25]

In the Fiscal Year 2010 NDAA, Congress directed DOD to develop and implement a new acquisition process for information technology systems that, among other things, include early and continuous involvement of the user.[26] This statute, in addition to DOD's 2010 report to Congress in response to the statute, and DODI 5000.02 identify characteristics of effective user engagement for DOD acquisitions, including:

- Early engagement: Users are involved early during development to ensure that efforts are aligned with user priorities.
- Continual engagement: Users are involved on a regular, recurring basis throughout development to stay informed about the system's technical possibilities, limitations, and development challenges.[27]
- Feedback based on actual working software: User feedback during development is based on usable software increments to provide early insight into the actual implementation of the solution and to test whether the design works as intended.
- Feedback incorporated into subsequent development: User feedback is incorporated into the next build or increment.[28]

---

[24] GAO-12-681.

[25] GAO-18-148.

[26] National Defense Authorization Act for Fiscal Year 2010, Pub. L. No. 111-84, § 804 (2009).

[27] Section 804's requirement for early and continual involvement of the user is consistent with the recommendations in Chapter 6 of the March 2009 report of the Defense Science Board Task Force, which notes that enhanced stakeholder engagement and analytical rigor should be throughout the acquisition life cycle. In earlier phases of the acquisition, the program reviews should be quarterly calendar-based events, while later phases should link such reviews with iterations or delivery of multiple, rapidly executed increments/releases of capability, among other things. See Defense Science Board, *Department of Defense Policies and Procedures for the Acquisition of Information Technology* (Washington, D.C.: March 2009).

[28] National Defense Authorization Act for Fiscal Year 2010, Pub. L. No. 111-84, § 804 (2009); Office of the Secretary of Defense Report to Congress, *A New Approach for Delivering*

Software Enables Operational Capability in All Segments of Space Systems

Defense space systems typically consist of multiple segments: one or more satellites, ground control systems, and, in some cases, terminals for end-users. Each segment depends on software to enable critical functionality, such as embedded software in satellite vehicles, in applications installed on computer terminals in ground control stations, or embedded signal processing software in user terminals to communicate with satellites, shown in Figure 5.

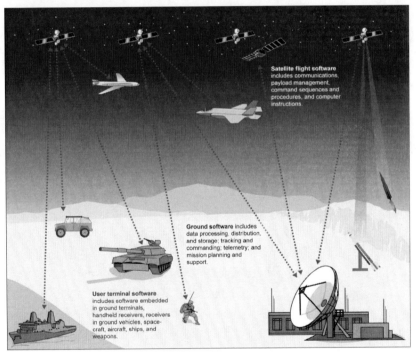

Source: GAO analysis of Department of Defense (DOD) documentation. | GAO-19-136.

Figure 5. Critical Software Functions within DOD Space Systems.

Information Technology Capabilities in the Department of Defense (Washington, D.C.: November 2010); DOD Instruction 5000.02, *Operation of the Defense Acquisition System* (Aug. 31, 2018).

74   *United States Government Accountability Office*

Selected Software-Intensive Space Systems Have a History of Cost Growth and Schedule Delays

We have previously reported on significant cost growth and schedule delays in numerous DOD space systems, with some space program costs rising as much as 300 percent, and delays so lengthy that some satellites spend years in orbit before key capabilities are able to be fully utilized.[29] In particular, the programs described below have experienced significant software challenges, including addressing cybersecurity requirements, which have contributed to cost growth and schedule delays.[30]

JOINT SPACE OPERATIONS CENTER (JSpOC) MISSION SYSTEM INCREMENT 2 (JMS)

The Air Force's JMS program aims to replace an aging space situational awareness and command and control system with improved functionality to better track and catalogue objects in the earth's orbit to support decision making for space forces. Increment 2 is to replace existing systems and deliver additional mission functionality. The Air Force is providing this functionality in three deliveries: the first delivery—Service Pack 7—provided hardware and software updates and was delivered in September 2014; the second delivery—Service Pack 9—aims to improve functions currently being performed, such as determining space object orbits and risks of collision; and the final delivery—Service Pack 11— aims to provide classified functionality.[31] The government is serving as the

---

[29] GAO, *Global Positioning System: Better Planning and Coordination Needed to Improve Prospects for Fielding Modernized Capability*, GAO-18-74 (Washington, D.C.: Dec. 12, 2017); and *Space Acquisitions: DOD Continues to Face Challenges of Delayed Delivery of Critical Space Capabilities and Fragmented Leadership*, GAO-17-619T (Washington, D.C.: May 17, 2017).

[30] In 2018, we reported extensively on DOD's challenges with addressing cybersecurity for weapon systems. GAO, *Weapon Systems Cybersecurity: DOD Just Beginning to Grapple with Scale of Vulnerabilities*, GAO-19-128 (Washington, D.C.: Oct. 9, 2018).

[31] The Air Force initially planned to deploy JMS as a single increment with five releases and final delivery in 2016. However, in 2011, we recommended, among other things, that DOD

DOD Space Acquisitions

system integrator directly managing the integration of government and commercially developed software onto commercial, off-the-shelf hardware, so there is no prime contractor.[32]

Historical software development challenges include:

- In 2015, we found that inconsistencies in the program's software development schedule made it unclear whether the program would be able to meet its remaining milestones.[33] The same year, the program declared a schedule breach against its baseline due, in part, to delays in resolving deficiencies identified during software testing.

- In 2016, DOD noted that the revised schedule was still highly aggressive with a high degree of risk because the program was concurrently developing and testing software.

- In 2017, developmental tests found a number of mission critical software deficiencies, which delayed operational testing. The Director of Operational Test and Evaluation also noted that additional work remained to help provide adequate cyber defense for JMS.

- During operational testing in 2018, JMS was found not operationally effective and not operationally suitable due, in part, to missing software requirements, urgent deficiencies that affected system performance, and negative user feedback.

---

ensure that key program risks are fully assessed to help ensure cost, schedule, and performance goals are met. We also noted in the report that implementing this recommendation may require dividing up the program into separate increments, which the Air Force later did in December 2011. See GAO, *Space Acquisitions: Development and Oversight Challenges in Delivering Improved Space Situational Awareness Capabilities*, GAO-11-545 (Washington, D.C.: May 27, 2011).

[32] According to the Air Force, the JMS program is transitioning to provide Space Situational Awareness and Battle Management Command and Control capabilities. For the purposes of this report, we reviewed JMS software development efforts through December 2018.

[33] GAO, *Defense Major Automated Information Systems: Cost and Schedule Commitments Need to Be Established Earlier*, GAO-15-282 (Washington, D.C.: Feb. 26, 2015).

JMS Inc. 2 Program Essentials

Source: U.S. Air Force. | GAO-19-136.

Program office:
  Air Force Space and Missile Systems Center, El Segundo, CA
Contractor:
  Government is directly managing the integration
Contract Type:
  Multiple support contracts
Software Development Approach:
  Agile Scrum
Operational Users:
  18th Space Control Squadron
  614th Air Operations Center
  National Space Defense Center
Start of System Development: June 2013
Cost at start of System Development (FY19$M): $1,005.82
Current Cost (FY19$M): $930.39[a]
First Estimated Date of Full Operational Capability: June 2016
Current Estimated Date of Full Operational Capability: TBD

Source: GAO analysis of Department of Defense data. | GAO-19-136.
[a] The current estimate reflects de-scoped requirements following a critical change reported to Congress in 2016, due to schedule delays of over 12 months that caused a cost increase of over 25 percent. The critical change reduced the scope and deferred some requirements to later phases in the program.

DOD Space Acquisitions 77

MOBILE USER OBJECTIVE SYSTEM (MUOS)

The Navy's MUOS program aims to provide satellite communications to fixed and mobile terminal users with availability worldwide. MUOS includes a satellite constellation, a ground control and network management system, and a new waveform for user terminals.[34] The ground system includes the ground transport, network management, satellite control, and associated infrastructure to both operate the satellites and manage the users' communications. The MUOS constellation is complete, and, according to program officials, software development officially ended in 2012 with the delivery of the waveform software. However, the user community still cannot monitor and manage MUOS. MUOS has two types of users: ground operators responsible for managing the MUOS communications network, and the military users of radios. Space and Missile Defense Command/Army Forces Strategic Command (SMDC/ARSTRAT) was the user representative while MUOS was developed.

While DOD allowed the program to move into sustainment—the phase after development is formally completed—the program continues to resolve challenges with the ground segment, and the contractor continues to deliver software updates to address deficiencies.[35] In 2017, the program transitioned its software sustainment efforts to an Agile development approach in preparation for a follow-on operational test currently scheduled to begin in June 2019. While Lockheed Martin Space Systems is the prime contractor for MUOS, we evaluated software efforts conducted by General Dynamics, the subcontractor performing software development.

Historical software development challenges include:

- In 2014, DOD found that 72 percent of the software was obsolete.

---

[34] Waveforms are software for end-user terminals.

[35] According to program officials, MUOS software has been in sustainment since 2012 but is funding ongoing software efforts as interim contractor support.

- Also in 2014, operational testing was delayed due to software reliability issues in the ground system and waveform.

MUOS Program Essentials

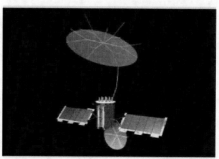

Source: © 2007 Lockheed Martin. | GAO-19-136.

Program office:
  Navy Space and Naval Warfare Systems Command, San Diego, CA
Contractor:
  Lockheed Martin Space Systems (Prime)
  General Dynamics (Software development subcontractor)
Contract Type:
  Cost Plus Incentive and Award Fee/Fixed Price Incentive (Firm Target) and Award Fee
Software Development Approach: Waterfall (Development)
  Scaled Agile Framework (Sustainment)
Operational Users:
  Naval Computer and Telecommunications Area Master Station Pacific (NCTAMS PAC)
  Space and Missile Defense Command/Army Forces Strategic Command (SMDC/ARSTRAT)
Start of System Development: Sept. 2004
Cost at start of System Development (FY19$M): $7,573.58
  Current Cost (FY19$M): $7,008.57[a]
First Estimated Date of Full Operational Capability: March 2014
Current Estimated Date of Full Operational Capability: April 2020

Source: GAO analysis of Department of Defense data. | GAO-19-136.
[a]The current estimate reflects a reduction of the MUOS satellite quantity from 6 to 5 satellites in 2015.

- In 2015, we found that over 90 percent of MUOS' planned capability was dependent on resolving issues related to integrating the MUOS waveform, terminals, and ground systems.[36]
- Also in 2015, operational tests determined MUOS was not operationally effective, suitable, or survivable due in part to cybersecurity concerns in the ground system.
- As of 2016, there were still existing and emerging cybersecurity vulnerabilities to be addressed.

NEXT GENERATION OPERATIONAL CONTROL SYSTEM (OCX)

The Air Force's OCX program is designed to replace the current ground control system for legacy and new GPS satellites. OCX software is being developed in a series of blocks: Block 0 is planned to provide the launch and checkout system and support initial testing of GPS III satellites and cybersecurity advancements. Blocks 1 and 2 are planned to provide command and control for previous generations of satellites and GPS III satellites as well as monitoring and control for current and modernized signals.[37] The OCX contractor delivered Block 0 in September 2017. The Air Force took possession of Block 0 in October 2017 by signing a certificate of conformance, and will accept it at a later date after Block 1 is delivered.[38]

---

[36] GAO, *Defense Acquisitions: Assessments of Selected Weapon Programs,* GAO-15-342SP (Washington, D.C.: Mar. 12, 2015).

[37] GAO has previously reported on OCX challenges. See, for example, GAO, *Weapon Systems Annual Assessment: Knowledge Gaps Pose Risks to Sustaining Recent Positive Trends,* GAO-18-360SP, (Washington, D.C.: Apr. 25, 2018); and *Global Positioning System: Better Planning and Coordination Needed to Improve Prospects for Fielding Modernized Capability,* GAO-18-74, (Washington, D.C.: Dec. 12, 2017).

[38] Per FAR § 46.504, a certificate of conformance may be used in certain instances instead of a source inspection at the discretion of a contracting officer if the following conditions apply: (a) acceptance on the basis of a contractor's certificate of conformance is in the Government's interest; (b)(1) small losses would be incurred in the event of a defect; (b)(2) because of the contractor's reputation or past performance, it is likely that the supplies or

Historical software development challenges include:

- In 2013, DOD paused OCX development due to incomplete systems engineering, which led to continuous rework and deferred requirements.

OCX Program Essentials

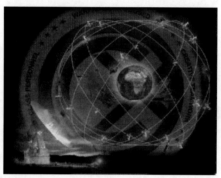

Source: U.S. Air Force. | GAO-19-136.

Program office:
Air Force Space and Missile Systems Center, El Segundo, CA
Contractor: Raytheon Contract Type:
Cost Plus Incentive Fee/Cost Plus Award Fee with Cost Plus Fixed Fee line items
Software Development Approach: Iterative-incremental; DevOps **Operational Users:** 2nd Space Operations Squadron
19th Space Operations Squadron
Start of System Development: Nov. 2012[a]
Cost at start of System Development (FY19$M): $3,730.89
Current Cost (FY19$M): $6,247.82
First Estimated Date of Transition to Operations: June 2017
Current Estimated Date of Transition to Operations: April 2022

Source: GAO analysis of Department of Defense data.| GAO-19-136.
[a]The Air Force awarded the OCX development contract to Raytheon in February 2010 before completing a milestone B decision formally authorizing the start of development in 2012.

---

services furnished will be acceptable and any defective work would be replaced, corrected, or repaired without contest.

DOD Space Acquisitions
81

- In 2015, we reported that, among other things, OCX had significant difficulties related to cybersecurity implementation.[39]
- In 2016, the program declared a Nunn-McCurdy unit cost breach.[40] Also in 2016, the contractor began implementing DevOps at the recommendation of Defense Digital Service but, according to the program office and contractor, only planned to automate development without the operations component of DevOps. The contractor did not achieve initial planned schedule efficiencies.
- In 2017, the Air Force accepted Block 0 despite over 200 open software defects. According to the program, when Block 0 was accepted there was also a plan to resolve the open software defects by the time of the first launch. Since then, according to the program office, all necessary defects related to launch have been addressed.
- In 2018, DOD noted that the schedule was at risk since the program made aggressive assumptions in its plan to develop, integrate, test software, and resolve defects.

SPACE-BASED INFRARED SYSTEM (SBIRS)

The Air Force's SBIRS program is an integrated system of both space and ground elements that aim to detect and track missile launches. SBIRS is designed to replace or incorporate existing defense support ground stations and satellites to improve upon legacy system timeliness, accuracy, and threat detection sensitivity. The Air Force is delivering the SBIRS ground system in one program with two increments: the first increment became operational in 2001 and supports functionality of existing satellites. The second increment, which is still in development, is designed

---

[39] GAO, *GPS: Actions Needed to Address Ground System Development Problems and User Equipment Production Readiness*, GAO-15-657, (Washington, D.C.: Sept. 9, 2015).

[40] 10 U.S.C. § 2433, commonly referred to as Nunn-McCurdy, requires the Department of Defense to notify Congress whenever a major defense acquisition program's unit cost experiences cost growth that exceeds certain thresholds.

82   *United States Government Accountability Office*

to provide new space segments, mission control software and hardware, and mobile ground capability.[41] The Air Force is delivering these capabilities in multiple blocks: Block 10 was accepted in 2016 and introduced new ground station software and hardware. Block 20 is expected to be complete by late 2019 and is planned to further improve ground station software.[42]

Historical software development challenges include:

- In 2001, 2002, and 2005, cost increases and schedule delays due, in part, to software complexity problems led to four separate Nunn-McCurdy unit cost breaches.
- In September 2007, we found that the amount of rework resulting from unresolved software discrepancies was contributing to cost growth and schedule delays.[43] In addition, the program had software algorithms that were not yet completed or demonstrated, hundreds of open deficiency reports, and a lack of coordination between space and ground system software databases.
- In 2016, DOD said that software deficiencies were contributing to delays in delivering the ground architecture.
- In 2018, DOD noted that flight software development remained a concern to the overall program schedule. According to SBIRS users and the program office, cybersecurity issues found during Block 10 testing are still being addressed as a part of the Block 20 effort.

---

[41] The initial SBIRS architecture included "High" and "Low" orbiting space-based components and ground processing segments. In 2001, the Low component was transferred from the Air Force to the Missile Defense Agency and was renamed the Space Tracking and Surveillance System. The Air Force continues to develop SBIRS High— Geosynchronous satellites (GEO) and Highly elliptical orbit (HEO) payloads—and related ground segment. For the purposes of this report, we evaluated software development in SBIRS ground and applicable flight software development.

[42] The reported costs include the baseline program (GEO 1-4, HEO 1-2 and ground) and the block buy program of GEO 5-6. The Air Force currently reports these programs separately.

[43] GAO, *Space Based Infrared System High Program and its Alternative,* GAO-07-1088R (Washington, D.C.: Sept. 12, 2007).

SBIRS Program Essentials

Source: U.S. Air Force. | GAO-19-136.

Program office:
   Air Force Space and Missile Systems Center,
   El Segundo, CA
Contractor:
   Lockheed Martin Space Systems
Contract Type:
   Fixed Price Incentive (Firm Target) with Cost Plus Fixed Fee line items
Software Development Approach:
   Incremental
Operational Users:
   460th Space Wing
Start of System Development: Oct. 1996
Cost at start of System Development (FY19$M): $5,467.97
Current Cost (FY19$M): $19,875.67
First Estimated Date of Full Operational Capability: N/A
Current Estimated Date of Full Operational Capability: N/A[a]

Source: GAO analysis of Department of Defense data. | GAO-19-136.
[a]The SBIRS program has not published objective or threshold Full Operational Capability dates.

SELECTED DOD SPACE PROGRAMS HAVE STRUGGLED TO INVOLVE USERS AND HAVE INFREQUENTLY DELIVERED SOFTWARE

DOD programs we reviewed frequently did not involve users early or continually during development, base user feedback on actual working software, or incorporate user feedback into subsequent software deliveries. Most programs had plans to incorporate these elements of user engagement throughout their software development efforts, but they often did not follow those plans due, in part, to the lack of specific guidance on user involvement and feedback. Regarding frequency of software delivery, while DODI 5000.02 suggests that programs deliver incremental software deliveries every 1 to 2 years, the programs we reviewed often continued to deliver software consistent with the long delivery schedules common to waterfall development. DOD is taking steps to address this issue.

Selected DOD Programs Often Did Not Effectively Engage Users

The four programs we reviewed often did not demonstrate key characteristics of effective user engagement as summarized below:

- Early engagement. OCX involved users early and JMS planned to involve users early but, in practice, did not do so; SBIRS and MUOS did not plan to involve users early in software development.
- Continual engagement. JMS, OCX, and SBIRS all planned to continually involve users but, in practice, did not fully do so; MUOS did not plan to do so.
- Feedback based on actual working software. OCX and SBIRS have provided users opportunities to provide such feedback but only years into software development; JMS and MUOS did not provide opportunities for feedback.

DOD Space Acquisitions   85

- Feedback incorporated into subsequent development. JMS, OCX, and SBIRS all planned to incorporate user feedback but, in practice, have not done so throughout development; MUOS did not plan to do so during software development.

Program efforts to involve users often did not match what their planning documentation described. In addition, when user input was collected, program officials did not capture documentation of how user feedback was addressed. Further, we found that, in practice, none of the programs we reviewed had users providing feedback on actual working software until years after system development began. This was the case even for programs utilizing Agile or iterative-incremental software development approaches, where user involvement and feedback from using functional systems early in the development cycle is foundational.

These shortcomings were due, in part, to the lack of specific guidance on user involvement and feedback. Both DODI 5000.02 and DOD's guiding principles for delivering information technology acquisitions note that software should be developed via usable software deliveries to obtain user acceptance and feedback for the next segment of work, but this guidance lacks specificity. In particular, DOD does not specify when to involve users and request their feedback, how frequently to seek user involvement and feedback on software deliverables, how to report back to users on how that feedback was addressed, and how to document the results of user involvement and feedback.[44]

As a result of programs' shortcomings with user involvement and feedback, programs risk delivering systems that do not meet user needs. In selected cases, delivered software was deemed operationally unsuitable by DOD testers and required substantial rework.

Further details on the extent to which programs implemented the four key characteristics are described below.

---

[44] DOD Instruction 5000.02, *Operation of the Defense Acquisition System* (Aug. 31, 2018); Office of the Secretary of Defense Report to Congress, *A New Approach for Delivering Information Technology Capabilities in the Department of Defense* (Washington, D.C.: November 2010).

JMS

Program documents created at the start of JMS system development contain specific operating procedures for conducting interactions with the user community—Air Force personnel who track and catalogue objects in orbit—during acquisition and fielding. However, the program has not followed these operating procedures during system development.

- Early Engagement. The JMS program office planned to involve users early in development but, in practice, did not do so. JMS program documentation states that users were to be involved in user engagement sessions within the first 4 weeks of iterative development.[45] However, the first documented user engagement session was held more than a year after development start.

- Continual Engagement. The JMS program office planned to engage users throughout development but, in practice, did not do so. JMS program documentation states that user engagement sessions are to be held regularly during development—roughly every 2 to 4 weeks. However, in practice, program officials told us they only involved users as needed during software development. We found that the frequency of user engagement events varied from several weeks to more than 6 months. According to program officials, there were limited users available, and their operational mission duties were prioritized over assisting with system development.

- Feedback Based on Actual Working Software. The JMS program office did not provide users an opportunity to give feedback based on actual working software during development. According to program documentation, designs and notional drawings, not working software, were to be used for user engagement sessions. While JMS did provide users opportunities to provide feedback, this feedback was not on actual working software. Program officials said the goal of these events was never intended to include

---

[45] According to JMS documentation, user engagement sessions are to be held within and associated with service pack sprints.

user feedback on actual working software. However, users told us that when they were finally able to use the system for the first time, 4 years after development started, it did not function as needed. The software did not execute what it had been designed to do, and earlier user engagement on actual working software may have identified these issues.

What is Operational Suitability?

Operational Suitability defines the degree to which a system is satisfactorily placed and operated in field use. Consideration for Operational Suitability includes, among other things:

- Reliability
- Availability
- Compatibility
- Transportability
- Interoperability
- Maintainability
- Safety
- Human Factors
- Manpower and Logistics Supportability
- Documentation
- Training Requirements

Source: GAO analysis of DOD and Industry Documentation | GAO-19-136.

- Feedback Incorporated Into Subsequent Development. The JMS program office planned to incorporate user feedback into development but, in practice, did not do so. JMS program documentation states that the program will document user feedback from user engagement events using summary notes communicated back to the user. However, JMS users said it was often unclear if their feedback was incorporated. For example, in March 2016, a user engagement event was held to discuss any questions and concerns relating to the planned system's conjunction assessment—a key feature that predicts orbit

88 *United States Government Accountability Office*

intersection and potential collision of space objects— that resulted in 8 user-identified issues. When we met with the users in 2018, they told us that conjunction assessment issues remained unaddressed, and they would still be reliant on the legacy system to fully execute the mission and perform their duties. The legacy system is still needed, they said, because the program deferred critical functions, and the most recent operational test found the system to be operationally unsuitable.

MUOS

The MUOS program office did not engage users—Army Forces Strategic Command personnel who support the narrowband and wideband communications across the Air Force, Marines, Navy, and Army—during software development but are engaging users while developing software during sustainment, the acquisition phase after development when the program mainly supports and monitors performance.[46] Following the end of development, at an operational test event in 2015, DOD testers deemed the system was operationally unsuitable. The MUOS program office moved to an Agile development approach in 2017 to address software deficiencies in preparation for the next operational test event.

- Early Engagement. The MUOS program office did not engage users early in development. Program documentation does not describe any plans for user engagement or involvement during development and, according to program officials, no users evaluated the actual system during development.

---

[46] For the purposes of this report, MUOS assessment reflects user engagement characteristics during software development, although the program has since incorporated Agile approaches during software sustainment. Since then, the program engages users on working software and incorporates their feedback into the next iteration of development. Space and Missile Defense Command/Army Forces Strategic Command (SMDC/ARSTRAT) represented military service users across the military components during MUOS system development, but not system operators at the Naval Computer and Telecommunications Area Master Station Pacific. According to program officials, there were no MUOS System Operators (Network Management personnel) with real world experience on a system like MUOS during development.

DOD Space Acquisitions

- Continual Engagement. The MUOS program office did not continually engage with users. Program documentation does not describe any plans for user engagement or involvement during development. Program officials said no users evaluated the system during development because there were no users with real world experience on a system like MUOS. However, as previously noted, SMDC/ARSTRAT represented end users' interests during MUOS development.

- Feedback Based on Actual Working Software. The MUOS program office did not provide users an opportunity to give feedback based on actual working software. Program documentation does not describe a process for obtaining user feedback based on actual working software. The first time users had a chance to fully operate the system was after development ended, in preparation for operational testing in 2014, which identified numerous defects. Additionally, MUOS users said that they have since identified 128 functions in 11 critical areas that must be addressed or they will not accept the system.[47] Users also said that some of the vulnerabilities found during operational testing, including cybersecurity vulnerabilities, have been deferred.

- Feedback Incorporated Into Subsequent Development. The MUOS program office did not incorporate user feedback into development. Program documentation did not describe plans to gain user feedback or acceptance into the development of the MUOS system. In addition, users and the contractor told us that program officials did not allow direct interaction during development due to a concern that such interactions could lead to changes in system requirements. The program office said that user involvement to-date has not caused delays to testing or software delivery.

---

[47] These items were based on a Joint MUOS Readiness Tracker, which was developed by both users and the program office to track all tasks that need to be completed across the program and operational command prior to full operational acceptance. The tasks are aligned to the system updates needed to return to operational test.

OCX

The OCX program had limited user engagement, but has recently held user engagement events based on releases of actual working software. The program has made efforts to obtain feedback from users, but users have noted there is no time in the schedule to address much of their feedback prior to delivering the system.

- Early Engagement. The OCX program office involved users early in development in accordance with its plans. From 2011, OCX users were involved in technical meetings where they provided feedback on the concept of operations and the design of the system.
- Continual Engagement. The OCX program office planned to engage users throughout development but, in practice, did not fully do so. OCX planning documentation includes multiple opportunities for user engagement at various stages of system development, including operational suitability and "hands-on" interaction with an integrated system.[48] According to the program office, numerous events were held for users to give feedback on the system. However, since 2012, the program has only held one of its planned events to address operational suitability. In addition, other opportunities for users to operate the system have been removed to accommodate the program's schedule, such as "day in the life" events that allowed users to validate the system as they would actually operate it. Users said that removing events like these created fewer opportunities to identify and resolve new deficiencies.
- Feedback Based on Actual Working Software. OCX did not plan to provide users an opportunity to give feedback based on actual working software but, in practice, did so years into development.

---

[48] According to the OCX Human Engineering Program Plan, comments are to be received from three primary event types or triggers: (1) active ("hands on") operator interaction on functional portions of OCX, or the integrated OCX system; (2) operator (non "hands on") participation in scheduled OCX operator engagement events; and stakeholder unsolicited recommendations.

OCX planning documents rely on simulations and mock-ups for evaluating system usability. However, users told us that mock-ups do not allow them to test functionality and may not be representative of the final delivered product. Starting in 2014—2 years after development started—users had opportunities to review the limited functionality available at the time. Since 2017, users said they were able to test working software.

- Feedback Incorporated Into Subsequent Development. The OCX program office planned to incorporate user feedback into development but, in practice, did not do so throughout development. OCX planning documentation includes a user comment response process that would collect and validate user comments and communicate results back to the users. According to the program office, for OCX Block 0, users provided feedback that was incorporated prior to the first launch. While OCX users said that they have the opportunity to provide feedback, there is a growing list of unaddressed Block 1 issues to be resolved. Some of these feedback points, if left unresolved, may result in operational suitability concerns and a delayed delivery to operations. According to the program office, critiques from the users have either been closed, incorporated into the OCX design, or are still under assessment between the contractor and users. A majority of user feedback points for the OCX iteration currently in development remain unresolved, as depicted in figure 6. In 2016, DOD told the Air Force and the contractor to utilize DevOps. As previously noted, DevOps is intended to release automated software builds to users in order to unify development and operations and increase efficiency. The contractor stated it implemented DevOps in 2016. However, both the Air Force and the contractor admitted in 2018 they never had plans to implement the "Ops" side of DevOps, meaning they didn't plan to automatically deliver software builds to the users. Without incorporating the users and experts in maintainability and deployment, the program is not benefiting from continuous user feedback.

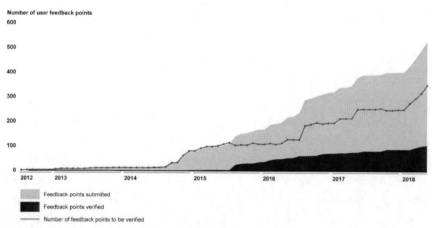

Source: GAO analysis of OCX data. | GAO-19-136.

Figure 6. Growing Backlog of OCX Operational Suitability Feedback Points from Users.

SBIRS

SBIRS users—Air Force personnel who operate, command, and control SBIRS satellites to detect and track missile launches—were not involved during early system development and the program only recently increased the frequency of user events. SBIRS users have been able to provide feedback on working software but are unaware how this feedback is incorporated into software development.

- Early Engagement. The SBIRS program office did not engage users early in development because users were not in place and user groups were not defined. The program planning documentation that instituted the framework for user involvement was not in place until 2004.[49] According to SBIRS users and test officials, this resulted in a poor interface design and users being

---

[49] The SBIRS Human Factors Engineering Program Plan was updated in 2004 to define the use of Operational Design Teams, which are used to apply user-centered design principles from the design effort through test, evaluation, and verification.

DOD Space Acquisitions

unable to respond adequately to critical system alerts when using the system. Though the program contractor told us that user involvement is critical for ensuring the developers deliver a system that users need and will accept, DOD officials said that users were not integrated with the development approach until the software was ready to be integrated into a final product.

- Continual Engagement. The SBIRS program office planned to engage users throughout development but, in practice, did not do so. SBIRS planning documentation includes users involved in regular working groups throughout development. SBIRS users began to be involved with system development in 2013 on a weekly basis. Users were not involved during the 17 years of system development prior to this time.

- Feedback Based on Actual Working Software. The SBIRS program did not plan to provide users an opportunity to give feedback based on actual working software during development but, in practice, did so years into development. SBIRS documentation only outlines user engagement as reviewing and commenting on design plans. While users were able to provide feedback on working software in 2017, these events did not occur until 21 years after the start of development when the software was ready to be integrated. When users were able to provide feedback, they identified issues with the training system and cybersecurity.

- Feedback Incorporated Into Subsequent Development. The SBIRS program planned to incorporate user feedback into development but, in practice, did not do so. SBIRS planning documentation includes methods for users to provide feedback, but users said there is no feedback loop between them and the developers; therefore, users are unaware if their comments and concerns are addressed or ignored.

94   *United States Government Accountability Office*

Selected Programs Have Generally Not Delivered Software Frequently, but DOD Is Taking Steps to Improve Efforts

DOD officials and DODI 5000.02 point to the benefits of delivering smaller packages of software more frequently, but the four programs we examined have generally delivered them infrequently. DOD is beginning to take steps to address these issues, such as establishing an independent advisory panel and considering recommendations issued by the Defense Science Board on the design and acquisition of DOD software.

Selected Programs Continue to Focus on Infrequent Deliveries

According to industry practices, short, quick deliveries allow a program to deliver useful, improved capabilities to the user frequently and continually throughout development. Within industry, iterations for Agile development approaches are typically up to 6 weeks, and working software is delivered to the user at the end of each iteration. In addition, DODI 5000.02 states that for incremental development increments should be delivered within 2 years.

While two programs in our review—JMS and MUOS—say they have undertaken elements of Agile development, which emphasize smaller deliveries of frequent software to users, they still struggled to move away from the long delivery schedules common to waterfall development. In addition, the two programs with incremental development—OCX and SBIRS—have not delivered within suggested DOD time frames.[50] See Figure 7 below for program software deliveries.

---

[50] DODI 5000.02 states that Incrementally Deployed Software Intensive Systems software deploys full capability in multiple increments as new capability is developed and delivered, nominally in 1-to 2-year cycles. DODI 5000.02, § 5(c)(3)(d) (Aug. 31, 2018). The OCX program is using an iterative-incremental software development approach. For the purposes of this review, we compared the program with both iterative and incremental recommended time frames.

DOD Space Acquisitions

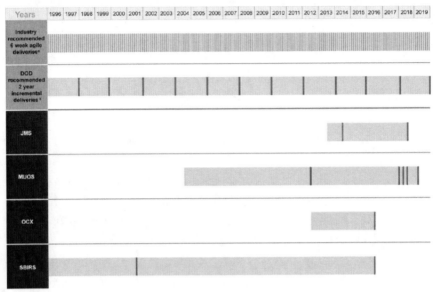

[a]Multiple industry recommend Agile deliveries within 1 to 6 weeks. We evaluated programs against the upper limit of this range.
JMS – Joint Space Operations Center Mission System
MUOS = Mobile User Objective System
OCX = Next Generation Operational Control System
SBIRS = Space-Based Infrared System
Source: GAO analysis of Department of Defense (DOD) and industry documentation. | GAO-10-136.

Figure 7. Selected Programs Are Not Delivering Software within Recommended Time Frames.

Further observations on each of the four programs follow:

- JMS program officials and documentation indicate that the program is using an Agile development approach to deliver smaller, rapid deliveries to minimize risk. According to JMS program documentation, software releases were to be delivered in 6-month intervals. However, the program only delivered actual working software once during development—a delivery of capability in 2014. The program was operationally accepted in late

2018. However, only 3 of 12 planned capabilities were accepted for operational use.

- The MUOS program used a traditional waterfall approach during development from 2004 to 2012 and has only had one overall software product delivery during that time. The program completed the software in 2012, yet continued to make changes during sustainment using the waterfall methodology and adopted an Agile approach in 2017 to address deficiencies. Since this adoption, it has delivered software more frequently—about every 3 months. This is a significant improvement over the delivery time frames during the MUOS waterfall development approach.
- The OCX program is using an "iterative-incremental" development approach. According to OCX software development plans, this approach was to enable early and frequent deliveries of capabilities. Specifically, the program plans for iterations to be completed every 22 weeks. However, since software development began in 2012, OCX has delivered just one increment of software, referred to by the OCX program as a block.
- The SBIRS program began in 1996, using a waterfall approach, and has had two deliveries of software. SBIRS Increment 1 was delivered in 2001, and the next increment, SBIRS Increment 2, Block 10, was delivered 15 years later, in 2016. The next increment, SBIRS Increment 2, Block 20, is expected to be delivered in 2019.

Part of the reason programs delivered larger software packages less frequently was the adherence to the process steps in the DODI 5000.02 that were designed under the waterfall approach. While DODI 5000.02 authorizes programs to tailor their acquisition procedures to more efficiently achieve program objectives, none of the programs that were trying to employ a newer development approach took steps to tailor procedures in order to facilitate development. For example, the OCX contractor said it was delayed by complying with technical reviews under a military standard for traditional waterfall approaches, such as the

Preliminary Design Review, Critical Design Review, and others, but the OCX program did not alter these reviews, despite having flexibility to do so. The contractor told us a more tailored approach would enable execution of smaller iterations of software deliverables. Similarly, the JMS program office noted that it was not fully able to integrate Agile development practices because of all the different technical reviews, but JMS did not tailor these requirements to more efficiently achieve outcomes, despite flexibility to do so.

DOD Officials Have Acknowledged These Challenges and Have Recently Begun Recommending Steps to Address Them

Officials we spoke with from Defense Digital Service, Director of Operational Test and Evaluation, and DOD leadership said that rapid development of software using newer software practices does not fit with the requirements of the DOD acquisition process. Further, DOD's Special Assistant for Software Acquisition said that DOD software development should be iterative, providing the critical capabilities in smaller, more frequent deliveries rather than delivering capabilities in a single delivery via traditional waterfall software development. In addition, other DOD officials we interviewed agreed that since DOD programs may not always know the full definition of a system's requirements until late in development, additional flexibility to tailor acquisition approaches could improve software acquisitions.

In acknowledging the challenges in moving from a waterfall model to a more incremental approach, various DOD groups have made recommendations to support delivery of smaller, more timely software deliverables:

- In February 2018, the Defense Science Board issued a series of recommendations to support rapid, iterative software development. The recommendations included requiring all programs entering system development to implement iterative approaches and providing authority to the program manager to work with users.[51]

- In April 2018, the Defense Innovation Board made recommendations to improve DOD software acquisitions, such as moving to more iterative development approaches that would deliver functionality more quickly.[52]

- In June 2018, the DOD Section 809 Panel recommended eliminating the requirements for Earned Value Management (EVM)—one of DOD's primary program planning and management tools—in Agile programs.[53] However, other DOD and industry guides state that Agile programs can still report EVM if certain considerations are made, such as an Agile work structure that provides a process for defining work and tracking progress of this work against planned cost and schedule.[54]

Pursuant to the Fiscal Year 2019 National Defense Authorization Act, DOD is required, subject to authorized exceptions, to begin implementation of each recommendation submitted in the final report of the Defense Science Board Task Force on the Design and Acquisition of Software for Defense Systems by February 2020. For each recommendation that DOD is implementing, it is to submit to the congressional defense committees a summary of actions taken; and a schedule, with specific milestones, for completing implementation of the recommendation.[55] We intend to monitor DOD's progress in implementing the recommendations.

---

[51] Department of Defense, Office of the Under Secretary of Defense for Research and Engineering, Defense Science Board, *Design and Acquisition of Software for Defense Systems* (February 2018).

[52] Department of Defense, Defense Innovation Board, *Ten Commandments of Software*, Version 0.14 (April 2018).

[53] Section 809 Panel, *Report of the Advisory Panel on Streamlining and Codifying Acquisition Regulations*, vol. 2 (June 2018).

[54] National Defense Industrial Association, *An Industry Practice Guide for Agile on Earned Value Management Programs*, Ver. 1.1 (2017).

[55] John S. McCain National Defense Authorization Act for Fiscal Year 2019, Pub. L. No. 115-232, § 868 (2018).

SELECTED PROGRAM OFFICES HAVE HAD SOFTWARE-SPECIFIC MANAGEMENT CHALLENGES BUT ARE TAKING STEPS TO ADDRESS WEAKNESSES

The programs we reviewed faced management challenges using commercial software, applying outdated software tools and metrics, and having limited knowledge and training in newer software development. DOD is taking steps to address these challenges.

Selected DOD Programs Face Difficulties Identifying the Effort Required by and Mitigating the Risk Associated with Commercial Software

DOD has previously encouraged DOD acquisition programs to use commercial software where appropriate. For example, in 2000 and in 2003, DOD policy encouraged considering the use of commercial software. In addition, regulations continue to emphasize consideration of commercial software suitable to meet the agency's needs in acquiring information technology. DOD officials said that, although the effort to maintain commercial software may be equivalent to developing such capabilities in-house, programs should still consider the use of commercial software because DOD and its contractors may lack the technical skillsets to develop a similar product.

What is Commercial Software?

Software that is ready-made and commercially available to the public.

Examples:
Microsoft Windows
Red Hat Enterprise Linux
VxWorks

Source: GAO Analysis of DOD and Industry Documentation | GAO-19-136.

United States Government Accountability Office

However, three of the programs we reviewed had difficulty integrating and maintaining modified commercial software during development:

- The JMS acquisition approach was to only use commercial and government-provided software with no new software development planned, but the commercial products selected were not mature and required additional development, contributing to schedule delays.

- The MUOS program underestimated the level of effort to modify commercial software, which increased cost and introduced schedule delays in completing both the ground system and the waveform. According to an Aerospace official who advised the program on software issues, the MUOS software development approach was to use a commercial software solution but with substantial modifications.[56] In particular, the MUOS contractor planned to take a commercial cellular system and substantially modify it for MUOS. This official, along with the MUOS program office, said that underestimating the level of effort to modify and integrate the commercial software has been the program's biggest challenge.

- In September 2015, we found that the OCX contractor was overly optimistic in its initial estimates of the work associated with incorporating open source and reused software. Further, according to the Air Force, OCX program managers and contractors did not appear to follow cybersecurity screening or software assurance processes as required.[57] For example, open source software was incorporated without ensuring that it was cybersecurity-compliant. These problems led to significant rework and added cost growth and schedule delays to address the cybersecurity vulnerabilities and meet cybersecurity standards. In addition, in an independent

---

[56] The Aerospace Corporation is a Federally Funded Research and Development Center (FFRDC). FFRDCs are unique nonprofit entities sponsored and funded by the U.S. government to meet some special long-term research or development need which cannot be met as effectively by existing in-house or contractor resources.

[57] GAO-15-657.

DOD Space Acquisitions

101

assessment of OCX, officials from the MITRE Corporation said that there is a lack of appreciation for the effort required for commercial software integration, stating that the level of effort is "categorically underestimated."[58]

Some program officials noted that commercial software updates led to system instability and increased costs. For example, OCX program officials said that updating an operating system version led to 38 other commercial software changes. Each of these changes had to be configured, which took considerable time and added cost to the program. Similarly, the SBIRS contractor said they have been concerned that updates to commercial software could create a domino effect of instability, and the risks could outweigh the benefits of the update. For example, if one commercial software product is updated and becomes unstable, instability may be introduced to other commercial software products and software components. On the other hand, not updating software products could lead to cybersecurity concerns. As we previously noted, developers of commercial software generally update software to address identified flaws and cybersecurity vulnerabilities.[59] We also reported in a review of weapon systems cybersecurity that, although there are valid reasons for delaying or forgoing weapon systems patches, this means some weapon systems are operating, possibly for extended periods, with known vulnerabilities.[60]

In addition, the lifecycles of commercial software can contribute to management challenges when these products become obsolete. For example, in 2014, a MUOS Ground System Deep Dive review identified that 72 percent of the MUOS software was considered to be obsolete.[61] According to program officials, commercial software became obsolete

---

[58] The MITRE Corporation is a FFRDC. In accordance with the Fiscal Year 2017 NDAA, MITRE conducted an Independent Program Assessment of the OCX program for DOD. National Defense Authorization Act for Fiscal Year 2017, Pub. L. No. 114-328, § 1622 (2016).

[59] GAO-19-128; and *Information Security: Effective Patch Management is Critical to Mitigating Software Vulnerabilities*, GAO-03-1138T (Washington, D.C.: Sept. 10, 2003).

[60] GAO-19-128.

[61] Obsolescence refers to the process or condition by which a piece of equipment, or software, becomes no longer useful, or a form and function which is no longer current; or is no longer supported by the supplier or original equipment manufacturer.

102 *United States Government Accountability Office*

before or soon after it was fielded, especially for operating systems and browsers, due to the long MUOS development cycle. Software obsolescence is also among the top risks of the OCX program and has contributed to additional costs during development.

DOD officials and others have started to acknowledge challenges in using commercial software. For example, as we previously reported in 2018, DOD has stated that many weapon systems rely on commercial and open source software and are subject to any cyber vulnerabilities that come with them.[62] While DOD states that using commercial software is a preferred approach to meet system requirements, some program officials we interviewed told us that the effort to modify and update commercial software is underestimated. DOD is working on helping programs understand commercial software risks. For example, in January 2018, DOD published a Guidebook for Acquiring Commercial Items. In addition, Defense Acquisition University offers several modules designed to address challenges in integrating commercial solutions.

Selected DOD Programs Are Using Outdated Software Tools and Metrics but Are Updating Them

Three of the DOD programs we reviewed have experienced challenges in using outdated software tools or identifying appropriate performance metrics as they transition to newer software development approaches.

What are Software Tools?

Software Tools: Tools to aid in the development of software code creation, integration, and testing.

Source: GAO analysis of Industry Documentation | GAO-19-136.

---

[62] GAO-19-128.

Contractors Continue to Rely upon Outdated Software Tools and Experience Challenges

We found that three of the programs we reviewed used tools that are considered outdated and lack the flexibility needed for iterative development. Contractors for three of the four programs we reviewed have experienced software development challenges due to outdated tools:

- The SBIRS contractor uses a suite of tools that is considered outdated for newer commercial approaches. For example, one of these tools relies on a central database that, if corrupted, will stop development work and could take days or weeks to fix. According to the contractor, fixing this database has led to multiple periods of downtime and schedule delays.
- The MUOS contractor also uses a toolset that is considered outdated by commercial software development experts. The program moved to a newer Agile development approach in 2017 but has retained an older software development toolset. The MUOS contractor said they are heavily reliant on these tools for development and do not anticipate changing the toolset.
- The OCX contractor also uses tools that are considered outdated by commercial approaches. According to the contractor, these tools have been in place for many years, and switching over to a new set of tools would not be in the best interest of the program because it could be disruptive to ongoing development. Defense Digital Service experts said that a particular suite of tools used by the OCX contractor is outdated because the tools lack the flexibility needed for iterative development.
- Both MUOS and SBIRS contractors said that they have had to train new employees to use their outdated tools. For example, the SBIRS contractor told us that when new employees begin work on the SBIRS program, they already know how to use newer tools but have to be trained on the outdated tools used for SBIRS

104   *United States Government Accountability Office*

development.[63] The SBIRS contractor said this has affected retention of its workforce in some cases, and the program has allocated funding to transition to newer tools in order to better recruit and retain personnel.

What is Cloud-Based Testing?

   Cloud-based testing uses cloud computing environments to simulate an application's real-world usage.

   According to international standards, cloud testing can lead to cost savings, improved testing efficiency, and more realistic testing environments.

Source: GAO analysis of Industry Documentation | GAO-19-136.

Two contractors have taken steps to update their software tools to increase automation and cloud-based testing but have not yet experienced the anticipated efficiencies:

- The OCX contractor is attempting to employ cloud-based testing and a DevOps approach. The contractor said it had to gain approval from the DOD Chief Information Office to employ commercial cloud-based testing for the unclassified portions of OCX but it has not gained similar approval for the classified portion.

- The SBIRS contractor is using a software testing tool that would allow for faster automated testing but is not yet realizing the full benefit of its use. The SBIRS testers did not use this tool in the way it was intended. Specifically, the contractor said that when the software was deployed to the testing environment, testers deactivated the software at the end of their shifts instead of allowing it to run continuously until the tests were complete. The contractor said the testers did this because there were concerns

---

[63] For example, newer software development practices use a set of tools such as configuration management software, continuous integration systems, code repositories, and issue tracking systems.

DOD Space Acquisitions   105

over unauthorized access to the system if no one was present. As a result, the contractor separated the tests into 8-hour segments rather than allowing the tests to run continuously, reducing the effectiveness and value of automated testing.

The Defense Science Board, Defense Innovation Board, and others have recommended DOD use tools that enable the developers, users, and management to work together daily. As noted, DOD is required to begin implementation of the recommendations made in the Defense Science Board report.

What are Software Metrics?

Software metrics are measurements which provide insight to the status and quality of software development.

Source: GAO analysis of Industry Documentation | GAO-19-136.

Metrics May Not Support Newer Development Approaches

We have previously found that leading developers track software-specific metrics to gauge a program's progress, and that traditional cost and schedule metrics alone may not provide suitable awareness for managing iterative software development performance.[64] Three programs have faced challenges in identifying and collecting metrics that provide meaningful insight into software development progress:

- JMS planned to collect traditional software development metrics to measure software size and quality, as well as Agile metrics that provide insight into development speed and efficiency. However, officials from the JMS government integrator managing sub-

---

[64] GAO, *Immigration Benefits System: U.S. Citizenship and Immigration Services Can Improve Program Management,* GAO-16-467 (Washington, D.C.: July 7, 2016); *Software Development: Effective Practices and Federal Challenges in Applying Agile Methods,* GAO-12-681 (Washington, D.C.: July 27, 2012); and Defense Acquisitions: *Stronger Management Practices Are Needed to Improve DOD's Software-Intensive Weapon Acquisitions,* GAO-04-393 (Washington, D.C: Mar. 1, 2004).

contracts said they lack regular reporting of metrics and access to data from subcontractors that would allow them to identify defects early. These officials said this was a challenge because the program has to run its own quality scans at the end of each sprint instead of being able to identify defects on a daily basis.

- MUOS program officials were able to receive Agile metrics from the contractor when they transitioned to Agile development, but they lacked access to the source data, which they said hindered their ability to oversee development.

- OCX program officials said they plan to use performance-based metrics throughout the remainder of the program. However, the metrics may not adequately track performance as intended. The Defense Contract Management Agency reviewed OCX metrics, particularly those related to DevOps, and expressed concern that program metrics may only measure total defects that were identified and corrected but may not provide insight into the complexity of those defects.

DOD Is Taking Steps to Identify Useful Software Development Metrics and Ways to Include Them in New Contracts

DOD is aware of challenges with metrics and is taking actions to address the issues. For example, the Defense Innovation Board is consulting with commercial companies to determine what metrics DOD should collect; and the Air Force's Space and Missile Systems Center has tasked The Aerospace Corporation with examining how to apply software performance metrics in contracts for DOD space programs. DOD offices such as the Defense Science Board and DOD Systems Engineering, as well as several Federally Funded Research and Development Centers including the Software Engineering Institute and The Aerospace Corporation, have also attempted to identify new metrics in correlation with advances in software development approaches.

Two Program Offices Lacked Newer Software Development Knowledge, but DOD Is Working to Improve Training

Two program offices we reviewed experienced challenges due to limited software development knowledge:

- OCX experienced an extended period of inefficient processes because it lacked an understanding of newer approaches. According to Defense Digital Service, when the Office of Secretary of Defense advised the OCX program in May 2016, it discovered that neither the program office nor contractor had been aware of the benefits of automated testing. Defense Digital Service helped the OCX contractor automate a process that had been taking as long as 18 months to one in which the same process takes less than a day. If the program office had been aware of newer software approaches, it could have recognized these inefficiencies much earlier and avoided unnecessary schedule delays.

- The MUOS contractor lacked an "Agile advocate" in the program office, which undermined its ability to fully employ an Agile development approach.[65] For example, even after the contractor adopted an Agile approach, the program office directed the contractor to plan out all work across software builds in order to maintain control over requirements—similar to a waterfall approach but inefficient in Agile. According to the Software Engineering Institute, without an Agile advocate in a program's leadership, organizations tend to do a partial Agile or "Agile-like" approach.[66]

---

[65] A practice of Agile development is to identify an Agile champion within senior management—someone with formal authority within the organization to advocate the Agile approach and resolve impediments. Similarly, another practice of Agile development is to ensure all teams include coaches or staff with Agile experience. This practice stresses the importance of including those with direct experience in applying Agile on each team.

[66] Software Engineering Institute, *Agile Software Teams: How They Engage with Systems Engineering on DoD Acquisition Programs,* Technical Note CMU/SEI-2014-TN-013 (July 2014).

108 *United States Government Accountability Office*

Program officials from the programs we reviewed said that while they have taken some software development training, more would be beneficial. The JMS program office said that there are external training courses available locally as well as trainings at Air Force's Space and Missile Systems Center, but neither are required. JMS program officials said that, while specific software training has not been required for the program outside of Defense Acquisition University certifications, courses on managing software-intensive programs would have been beneficial. Similarly, Defense Contract Management Agency officials told us that OCX program officials would have benefited from more software development training. The MUOS program office said its training on software acquisition, software and systems measurement, software planning supportability and cost estimating, and software policies and best practices was sufficient, but the program office did not have newer software development training prior to transitioning to an Agile development approach.

DOD is working to improve software acquisition training requirements and update them to reflect changes in the software development industry. For example, in 2017, the Defense Acquisition University introduced a course on Agile software development that includes how Agile fits into the overall Defense Acquisition System and how to manage an Agile software development contract. DOD told us it is also working with the Defense Acquisition University to help inform a course on DevOps automation.

CONCLUSION

Software is an increasingly important enabler of DOD space systems. However, DOD has struggled to deliver software-intensive space programs that meet operational requirements within expected time frames. Although user involvement is critical to the success of any software development effort, key programs often did not effectively engage users. Program efforts to involve users and incorporate feedback frequently did not match plans. This was due, in part, to the lack of specific guidance on the timing, frequency, and documentation for user involvement and feedback. The lack of user engagement has contributed to systems that were later found to be operationally unsuitable.

Selected programs have also faced challenges in delivering software in shorter time frames, and in using commercial software, applying outdated software tools and metrics, and having limited knowledge and training in newer software development techniques. DOD acknowledges these challenges and is taking steps to address them.

RECOMMENDATIONS FOR EXECUTIVE ACTION

We are making the following two recommendations to DOD:

The Secretary of Defense should ensure the department's guidance that addresses software development provides specific, required direction on when and how often to involve users so that such involvement is early and continues through the development of the software and related program components. (Recommendation 1)

The Secretary of Defense should ensure the department's guidance that addresses software development provides specific, required direction on documenting and communicating user feedback to stakeholders during software system development. (Recommendation 2)

AGENCY COMMENTS AND OUR EVALUATION

We provided a draft of this product to the Department of Defense for comment. In its comments, reproduced in appendix II, DOD concurred. DOD also provided technical comments, which we incorporated as appropriate.

We are sending copies of the report to the Acting Secretary of Defense; the Secretaries of the Army, Navy, and Air Force; and interested congressional committees.

110 *United States Government Accountability Office*

Jon Ludwigson
Acting Director, Contracting and National Security Acquisitions

List of Committees

The Honorable James M. Inhofe
Chairman

The Honorable Jack Reed
Ranking Member
Committee on Armed Services
United States Senate

The Honorable Richard Shelby
Chairman

The Honorable Richard Durbin
Ranking Member Subcommittee of Defense
Committee on Appropriations
United States Senate

The Honorable Adam Smith
Chairman

The Honorable Mac Thornberry
Ranking Member
Committee on Armed Services
House of Representatives

The Honorable Peter Visclosky
Chairman

The Honorable Ken Calvert
Ranking Member Subcommittee of Defense
Committee on Appropriations
House of Representatives

APPENDIX I: OBJECTIVES, SCOPE, AND METHODOLOGY

Senate and House reports accompanying the National Defense Authorization Act for Fiscal Year 2017 contained provisions for GAO to review challenges in software-intensive Department of Defense (DOD) space systems, among other things. This report addresses, for selected software-intensive space programs, (1) the extent to which these programs have involved users and delivered software using newer development approaches; and (2) what software-specific management challenges, if any, these programs have faced.

To select the programs, we identified a non-generalizable, purposeful sample of four major defense programs representing different space military services where software is an essential component and where each program has experienced cost growth or schedule delays attributed, in part, to software challenges. We began our selection process with 49 DOD space programs from the U.S. Air Force and Navy services as identified by the Office of the Assistant Secretary of the Air Force for Space Acquisition and a GAO subject matter expert. We then narrowed our selection to 19 Major Defense Acquisition Programs (MDAP) and Major Acquisition Information System (MAIS) programs identified by DOD. Next, using information from prior GAO Annual Weapons Assessments, DOD Selected Acquisition Reports, DOD Defense Acquisition Executive Summary Reports, and the Defense Acquisition Management Information Retrieval system, we identified 15 programs that were software-intensive systems as defined in the international standard ISO/IEC/IEEE 42207. This standard states that a software-intensive system is one where software contributes essential influences to the design, construction, deployment, and evolution of the system as a whole. From these 15 programs, 8 were

112 *United States Government Accountability Office*

found to have had cost growth or schedule delays attributed, in some part, to software development.[67] We further analyzed these 8 programs for unit cost or schedule breaches as defined in 10 U.S.C. § 2433 and 10 U.S.C. § 2366b, ultimately resulting in 7 programs.[68] Finally, from these 7 programs, we chose a purposeful sample of 5 programs, ensuring representation from different DOD services and Acquisition Categories.

These programs are:

- Family of Advanced Beyond Line-of-Sight Terminals (FAB-T); Air Force MDAP
- Next Generation Operational Control System (OCX); Air Force MDAP
- Joint Space Operations Center Mission System Increment 2 (JMS); Air Force MAIS
- Mobile User Objective System (MUOS); Navy MDAP
- Space-Based Infrared System (SBIRS); Air Force MDAP

---

[67] These cost and schedule breaches are, or in the case of schedule breaches, were, defined as: Significant Nunn-McCurdy Unit Cost Breach: The cost growth threshold, as it relates to the current Acquisition Performance Baseline, is an increase of at least 15 percent over the program acquisition unit cost (PAUC) or average procurement unit cost (APUC) for the current program as shown in the current Baseline Estimate. The cost growth threshold, as it relates to the original Acquisition Performance Baseline, is an increase of at least 30 percent over the PAUC or APUC for the original program as shown in the original Baseline Estimate. Significant Change, as it relates to the original estimate: schedule change that will cause a delay of more than 6 months but less than 1 year; an increase in the estimated development cost or full life-cycle cost for the program by at least 15 percent but less than 25 percent; or a significant, adverse change in the expected performance of the MAIS to be acquired. Critical Change, as it relates to the original estimate: the system has failed to achieve a Full Deployment Decision within 5 years after the Milestone A decision for the program or, if there was no Milestone A, the date when the preferred alternative is selected for the program (excluding any time during which program activity is delayed as a result of a bid protest); a schedule change will cause a delay of 1 year or more; the estimated development cost or full life-cycle cost for the program has increased 25 percent or more; or a change in expected performance will undermine the ability of the system to perform the functions anticipated (i.e., the expected failure to meet a threshold Key Performance Parameter).

[68] The MDAP definitions for significant and critical unit cost breaches are based on unit cost growth as defined in 10 U.S.C. § 2433. The MAIS program definitions for significant and critical changes are based on schedule, cost, or expected performance of the program were defined in 10 U.S.C. 2445c prior to repeal by the National Defense Authorization Act for Fiscal Year 2010, Pub. L. No. 111-84, § 846 (2009).

We were unable to assess FAB-T software issues with the same level of detail as the other programs we reviewed because, despite prior software challenges, the program stated it does not have documentation that separately tracks software-related requirements or efforts. This brought our total to 4 selected programs.

To address the objectives, we interviewed officials from the Undersecretary of Defense for Acquisition and Sustainment, Office of the Deputy Assistant Secretary of Defense for Systems Engineering, Office of Cost Assessment and Program Evaluation, Office of the Director of Operational Test and Evaluation, Defense Digital Service, Defense Innovation Board, and the Office of the Assistant Secretary of the Air Force for Space Acquisition. We also interviewed officials from the selected program offices and their respective contractors, subcontractor, integrator, space systems users, a DOD test organization, and Federally Funded Research and Development Centers. In addition, we conducted a literature search using a number of bibliographic databases, including ProQuest, Scopus, DIALOG, and WorldCat. We reviewed documentation that focused on software-intensive major military acquisitions. We conducted our search in March 2018.

To determine how effectively selected DOD software-intensive space programs have involved users and adopted newer software development approaches, we reviewed applicable DOD policies, guidance, and federal statute that identify characteristics of user engagement. These sources were the Department of Defense Instruction (DODI) 5000.02; Office of the Secretary of Defense Report to Congress, *A New Approach for Delivering Information Technology in the Department of Defense;* and National Defense Authorization Act for Fiscal Year 2010. We supplemented this with Defense Science Board and Defense Innovation Board documentation, and other industry analyses. We then reviewed relevant program plans and documentation, such as human engineering and human systems integration plans, standard operating procedures, acquisition strategies, software development plans, and other program user engagement guidance to identify plans for user engagement. We then conducted interviews with space system users and analyzed software

114 *United States Government Accountability Office*

development documentation to evaluate the extent to which programs met these DOD user engagement characteristics. We also analyzed user feedback reports to identify trends in user feedback. We also examined DOD and OMB guidance and applicable leading practices to identify time frames for delivering software under incremental and iterative software development approaches, and we compared these time frames to program performance.

To determine what software-specific management challenges, if any, selected programs faced, we reviewed reports and studies on software tools and metrics used to manage software programs, including GAO reports,[69] DOD policies and guidance,[70] and studies from the Software Engineering Institute.[71] We then reviewed program documents, such as Software Development Plans, System Engineering Plans, System Engineering Management Plans, Software Resource Data Reports, Test and Evaluation Master Plans, Master Software Build Plans, and Obsolescence Plans, as applicable, as well as contracts and Statements of Work. We reviewed

---

[69] GAO, Immigration Benefits System: *U.S. Immigration Services Can Improve Program Management*, GAO-16-467 (Washington, D.C.: July 7, 2016); *Standards for Internal Control in the Federal Government*, GAO-14-704G, (Washington, D.C.: September 2014); *Software Development: Effective Practices and Federal Challenges in Applying Agile Methods*, GAO-12-681 (Washington, D.C.: July 27, 2012); *Information Technology: Critical Factory Underlying Successful Major Acquisitions*, GAO-12-7 (Washington, D.C.: Oct. 21, 2011); and *Defense Acquisitions: Stronger Management Practices Are Needed to Improve DOD's Software Intensive Weapon Acquisitions*, GAO-04-393 (Washington, D.C.: Mar. 1, 2004).

[70] DOD Instruction 5000.02, *Operation of the Defense Acquisition System*, (Aug. 31, 2018); DOD 5000.4-M-2, *Software Resources Data Report (SRDR) Manual*, (February 2004); ISO/IEC/IEEE 12207, *International Standard: Systems and Software Engineering—Software Life Cycle Processes*, ISO/IEC/IEEE 12207:2017(E), (November 2017); Office of the Assistant Secretary of the Navy (Research, Development and Acquisition), *Guidebook for Acquisition of Naval Software Intensive Systems*, (September 2008); Office of the Assistant Secretary of the Navy (Research, Development and Acquisition), *Software Criteria and Guidance for Systems Engineering Technical Reviews (SETR)*, (September 2010); Air Force Space Command Space and Missile Systems Center Standard, Software *Development*, SMC-S-012, (Jan. 16, 2015).

[71] Software Engineering Institute, *DOD Software Factbook: Software Engineering Measurement and Analysis Group, Version 1.1*, (December 2015); Software Engineering Institute, *Isolating Patterns of Failure in Department of Defense Acquisition*, Technical Note CMU/SEI-2013-TN-014, (June 2013); Software Engineering Institute, *Using Software Development Tools and Practices in Acquisition*, Technical Note CMU/SEI-2013-TN-017, (December 2013); Software Engineering Institute, *Agile Metrics: Progress Monitoring of Agile Contractors*, Technical Note CMU/SEI-2013-TN-029; (January 2014).

defect metrics and reports on amounts of new, reused, inherited, and commercial software; test and evaluation reports; program management reports; and external program assessments. We also evaluated program retrospectives and DOD reports on leading practices to understand how programs are making efforts to address challenges in these areas. We spoke with contractors and an applicable subcontractor and government integrator, program officials, and officials from Federally Funded Research and Development Centers to understand program issues, including program office and contractor training requirements.

We conducted this performance audit from November 2017 to March 2019 in accordance with generally accepted government auditing standards. Those standards require that we plan and perform the audit to obtain sufficient, appropriate evidence to provide a reasonable basis for our findings and conclusions based on our audit objectives. We believe that the evidence obtained provides a reasonable basis for our findings and conclusions based on our audit objectives.

APPENDIX II: COMMENTS FROM THE DEPARTMENT OF DEFENSE

ASSISTANT SECRETARY OF DEFENSE
3600 DEFENSE PENTAGON
WASHINGTON, DC 20301-3600

ACQUISITION

January 23, 2019

Mr. Jon Ludwigson
Acting Director, Contracting and National Security Acquisitions
U.S. Government Accountability Office
441 G Street, N.W.
Washington, DC 20548

Dear Mr. Ludwigson:

(U) This is the Department of Defense (DoD) response to the GAO Draft Report, GAO-19-136, "DOD SPACE ACQUISITIONS: Including Users Early and Often in Software Development Could Benefit Programs," dated December 20, 2018 (GAO Code 102475).

116   *United States Government Accountability Office*

Sincerely,

Kevin Fahey

**GAO Draft Report Dated December 20, 2018
GAO-19-136 (GAO CODE 102475)**

**"DOD SPACE ACQUISITIONS: INCLUDING USERS EARLY AND OFTEN IN
SOFTWARE DEVELOPMENT COULD BENEFIT PROGRAMS"**

**DEPARTMENT OF DEFENSE COMMENTS
TO THE GAO RECOMMENDATION**

RECOMMENDATION 1: The Secretary of Defense should ensure the department's guidance that addresses software development provides specific, required direction on when and how often to involve users so that such involvement is early and continues through the development of the software and related program components.

DoD RESPONSE: DoD concurs.

RECOMMENDATION 2: The Secretary of Defense should ensure the department's guidance that addresses software development provides specific, required direction on documenting and communicating user feedback to stakeholders during software system development.

DoD RESPONSE: DoD concurs.

APPENDIX III: ACCESSIBLE DATA

Data Tables

Data Table for Figure 6: Growing Backlog of OCX Operational Suitability Feedback Points from Users

Year	Data	Feedback points verified	Feedback points submitted	Number of feedback points to be verified
2012	J	0	0	0
	A	0	1	1
	S	0	1	1
	O	0	1	1
	N	0	1	1
	D	0	1	1

Year	Data	Feedback points verified	Feedback points submitted	Number of feedback points to be verified
2013	J	0	4	4
	F	0	6	6
	M	0	6	6
	A	0	6	6
	M	0	6	6
	J	0	6	6
	J	0	8	8
	A	0	9	9
	S	0	9	9
	O	0	9	9
	N	0	10	10
	D	0	10	10
2014	J	0	10	10
	F	0	10	10
	M	0	10	10
	A	0	10	10
	M	0	10	10
	J	0	11	11
	J	0	11	11
	A	0	13	13
	S	0	28	28
	O	0	29	29
	N	0	55	55
	D	1	74	73
2015	J	1	74	73
	F	1	84	83
	M	2	91	89
	A	2	91	89
	M	2	94	92
	J	2	101	99
	J	2	106	104
	A	23	117	94
	S	27	123	96
	O	29	124	95
	N	29	132	103
	D	34	133	99
2016	J	35	133	98
	F	42	144	102
	M	46	144	98
	A	47	149	102
	M	51	167	116
	J	52	168	116
	J	60	175	115

118   *United States Government Accountability Office*

(Continued)

Year	Data	Feedback points verified	Feedback points submitted	Number of feedback points to be verified
2016	A	60	227	167
	S	61	233	172
	O	62	241	179
	N	68	242	174
2017	D	70	248	178
	F	72	266	194
	M	72	267	195
	A	75	270	195
	M	75	304	229
	J	80	310	230
	J	80	310	230
	A	80	310	230
	S	80	313	233
	O	87	313	226
	N	87	313	226
	D	87	315	228
2018	J	87	315	228
	F	87	339	252
	M	95	364	269
	A	101	391	290
	M	104	423	319

INDEX

A

agencies, 2, 4, 8, 11, 15, 19, 21, 23, 24, 26, 28, 29, 30, 31, 33, 34, 36, 38, 40, 45, 46, 49, 53, 54, 55, 56, 62, 66

Air Force, 59, 64, 74, 75, 76, 79, 80, 81, 82, 83, 86, 88, 91, 92, 100, 106, 108, 109, 111, 112, 113, 114

B

benefits, 9, 11, 12, 17, 18, 48, 94, 101, 107
Bureau of Justice Statistics, 8, 10, 11, 26
businesses, 4, 11, 28

C

challenges, viii, 59, 60, 61, 63, 64, 65, 72, 74, 75, 77, 79, 80, 82, 97, 99, 101, 102, 103, 105, 106, 107, 109, 111, 113, 114
commercial, 3, 5, 11, 14, 15, 18, 25, 32, 37, 60, 75, 99, 100, 101, 102, 103, 104, 106, 109, 115
community, 27, 29, 77, 86

Congress, iv, 2, 5, 18, 26, 27, 35, 36, 47, 49, 55, 62, 64, 72, 76, 81, 85, 113
Consolidated Appropriations Act, 33
consumer advocates, 51
consumer education, 7, 15, 16, 17, 20, 24, 26, 28, 30, 31, 38, 39
consumer protection, 6, 38, 56
consumers, vii, 2, 3, 4, 5, 6, 8, 10, 11, 12, 13, 14, 15, 16, 17, 18, 19, 21, 22, 23, 24, 25, 26, 27, 29, 30, 31, 35, 36, 37, 40, 46, 47, 48, 50, 52, 54, 55, 56
cost, viii, 2, 12, 13, 16, 17, 21, 23, 25, 31, 34, 35, 58, 59, 61, 63, 64, 74, 75, 76, 81, 82, 98, 100, 101, 104, 105, 108, 111, 112
credit and debit card, 9
credit card fraud, 28
credit market, 14
creditors, 11, 20, 27
creditworthiness, 22
customers, 14, 15, 25
cybersecurity, 74, 79, 81, 82, 89, 93, 100, 101

D

data breach risks, vii, 2, 13, 16

120 *Index*

data breaches, v, vii, 1, 2, 3, 5, 6, 8, 12, 13, 14, 15, 18, 24, 26, 27, 28, 30, 31, 32, 33, 34, 35, 37, 40, 46, 54, 55
data collection, 55
database, 8, 15, 34, 103
defects, 81, 89, 106
deficiencies, 61, 71, 75, 77, 82, 88, 90, 96
Department of Defense (DOD), v, viii, 32, 57, 58, 59, 60, 61, 62, 63, 64, 65, 66, 67, 68, 69, 70, 71, 72, 73, 74, 75, 76, 77, 78, 80, 81, 82, 83, 84, 85, 87, 88, 91, 93, 94, 95, 97, 98, 99, 101, 102, 104, 105, 106, 107, 108, 109, 111, 113, 114
Department of Justice, 8, 11, 26, 29, 30

E

education, 7, 30, 38, 39
employees, 7, 15, 31, 32, 33, 103
employers, 22
employment, 6, 8, 10, 24
enforcement, 46, 48, 51, 52, 53, 55
engineering, 61, 65, 80, 113
evidence, 6, 7, 16, 40, 46, 65, 115
Executive Order, 7, 26, 29, 30, 39
exposure, 5, 6, 8, 10, 27, 30, 37

F

federal assistance, 4, 5, 37
Federal Communications Commission, 46
federal government, 7, 9, 19, 30, 39, 55, 114
federal law, 4
financial, 3, 5, 7, 8, 9, 10, 11, 13, 18, 19, 25, 27, 29, 30, 35, 39, 45, 47, 55
financial institutions, 11, 19, 25, 27, 29, 30
fraud, 3, 5, 6, 8, 9, 10, 11, 12, 13, 14, 15, 18, 19, 20, 21, 22, 23, 25, 27, 28, 29, 30, 31, 34, 35, 37, 39, 40, 55

G

gambling, 18
growth, viii, 58, 59, 61, 63, 64, 74, 81, 82, 100, 111, 112
guidance, viii, 2, 4, 15, 26, 33, 34, 40, 59, 60, 62, 64, 65, 66, 68, 69, 84, 85, 108, 109, 113, 114
guiding principles, 85

H

health, 9, 11, 16, 18, 47
health care, 16
health insurance, 11, 18
House of Representatives, 4, 110, 111

I

identity, vii, 2, 3, 4, 5, 6, 8, 9, 10, 11, 12, 13, 14, 15, 16, 17, 18, 19, 20, 23, 25, 26, 27, 28, 29, 30, 31, 32, 33, 34, 35, 36, 37, 38, 39, 40, 54, 55
identity theft, v, vii, 1, 2, 3, 5, 6, 7, 8, 9, 10, 11, 12, 13, 14, 15, 16, 17, 18, 19, 20, 23, 25, 26, 27, 28, 29, 30, 31, 32, 33, 34, 35, 36, 37, 38, 39, 40, 41, 54, 55
identity theft service providers, vii, 2, 6, 15, 18, 19, 29, 33, 37, 38, 39
individuals, 2, 3, 6, 7, 9, 10, 12, 14, 15, 16, 20, 23, 27, 28, 31, 32, 33, 35, 36, 37, 39, 40, 47, 52, 69
industry, vii, 2, 3, 6, 9, 12, 14, 15, 16, 17, 18, 20, 22, 23, 25, 29, 37, 38, 41, 42, 43, 44, 45, 46, 51, 52, 54, 55, 56, 59, 61, 65, 66, 67, 68, 69, 70, 71, 94, 95, 98, 108, 113
information security, vii, 1, 101
information technology, 62, 66, 68, 72, 85, 99

Index

integration, 65, 67, 70, 71, 75, 76, 101, 102, 104, 113

issues, vii, 2, 5, 10, 15, 26, 29, 31, 37, 45, 64, 78, 79, 82, 87, 88, 91, 93, 94, 100, 106, 113, 115

iteration, 69, 88, 91, 94

L

law enforcement, 27, 29, 30, 48

laws, 9, 27, 29, 31, 45, 47

laws and regulations, 29, 31

legislation, 2, 5, 20, 34, 47, 55, 62

M

management, viii, 34, 59, 61, 62, 63, 65, 77, 98, 99, 101, 104, 105, 107, 111, 114

medical, 3, 9, 11, 18, 28, 53

medical care, 3

mental health, 18

military, 23, 61, 62, 77, 88, 96, 111, 113

misuse, 8, 15, 18, 25, 47

mobile phone, 10, 11, 19, 24

N

National Defense Authorization Act, viii, 58, 62, 63, 64, 72, 98, 101, 111, 112, 113

National Retail Federation, 38

O

officials, viii, 6, 27, 40, 46, 53, 59, 64, 65, 71, 77, 85, 86, 88, 89, 92, 94, 95, 97, 99, 101, 102, 105, 106, 108, 113, 115

operating system, 101, 102

operations, 67, 70, 81, 90, 91

opportunities, 35, 51, 60, 84, 86, 90, 91

oversight, 46, 51, 52, 53, 62

P

policy, 6, 9, 27, 33, 34, 37, 50, 60, 64, 99

preparation, iv, 50, 77, 88, 89

protection, 12, 15, 19, 23, 24, 47, 48, 53

R

recommendations, iv, 7, 33, 35, 37, 40, 59, 64, 72, 90, 94, 97, 98, 105, 109

regulations, 29, 49, 50, 51, 53, 54, 99

requirements, 15, 23, 24, 49, 50, 51, 52, 61, 62, 64, 68, 72, 74, 75, 76, 80, 89, 97, 98, 102, 107, 108, 113, 115

research institutions, 37

researchers, 14, 19

resolution, 61

resources, 7, 26, 27, 30, 31, 33, 39, 100

response, 12, 14, 33, 34, 35, 36, 55, 63, 64, 70, 72, 91

restoration, 3, 12, 14, 17, 18, 26, 31, 32, 33, 40

risk, vii, 2, 3, 4, 5, 12, 13, 14, 16, 18, 19, 25, 27, 30, 31, 34, 35, 36, 55, 60, 62, 72, 74, 75, 81, 85, 95, 101, 102

risk management, 62

risks of harm, vii, 2, 4, 5, 19

S

schedule delays, viii, 58, 59, 61, 63, 74, 76, 82, 100, 103, 107, 111

Secretary of Defense, 63, 64, 71, 72, 85, 98, 107, 109, 113

security, 4, 7, 11, 12, 17, 19, 27, 29, 30, 39, 45, 48, 49, 53, 54, 55

security practices, 12

self-monitoring, 18, 20

service provider, vii, 2, 6, 15, 17, 18, 19, 29, 31, 33, 37, 38, 39, 48

Index

services, iv, 2, 3, 5, 6, 9, 10, 11, 12, 13, 14, 15, 16, 17, 18, 19, 20, 25, 26, 31, 32, 33, 34, 35, 37, 38, 40, 45, 47, 50, 55, 56, 63, 64, 80, 111

Social Security, 3, 5, 8, 9, 12, 16, 17, 18, 25, 29, 30

Social Security Administration, 9, 13, 29, 30

software, viii, 58, 59, 60, 61, 62, 63, 64, 65, 66, 67, 68, 69, 70, 71, 72, 73, 74, 75, 77, 78, 79, 80, 81, 82, 84, 85, 86, 88, 89, 90, 91, 92, 93, 94, 95, 96, 97, 98, 99, 100, 101, 102, 103, 104, 105, 106, 107, 108, 109, 111, 113, 114

software-intensive DOD space programs, viii, 59

software-intensive space systems, viii, 58, 74

solution, 3, 16, 20, 72, 100

space defense programs, viii, 59

space system acquisitions, viii, 58, 61

space systems, viii, 59, 61, 64, 73, 74, 77, 78, 83, 108, 111, 113

T

technical comments, 36, 109

testing, 29, 39, 61, 66, 70, 72, 75, 78, 79, 82, 89, 102, 104, 107

theft, vii, 2, 3, 5, 6, 7, 8, 9, 10, 11, 12, 13, 14, 15, 16, 17, 18, 19, 20, 23, 25, 26, 27, 28, 29, 30, 31, 32, 33, 34, 35, 36, 37, 38, 39, 40, 54, 55

time frame, 65, 94, 96, 108, 109, 114

training, 34, 61, 62, 71, 93, 99, 108, 109, 115

U

United States, v, vii, 1, 45, 54, 57, 110

user engagement, viii, 59, 60, 64, 66, 72, 84, 86, 87, 88, 89, 90, 93, 109, 113

V

victims, 3, 8, 10, 11, 12, 23, 25, 26, 28, 30

W

websites, 12, 15, 20, 30, 38, 46, 50

workforce, 104

working groups, 93

worldwide, 77

Related Nova Publications

Security and Authentication: Perspectives, Management and Challenges

Editors: Ong Thian Song, Tee Connie and Mohd Shohel Sayeed

Series: Cybercrime and Cybersecurity Research

Book Description: This book presents the current popular issues in information security and privacy, covering human users, hardware and software, the Internet and also communication protocols. The book provides a comprehensive combination of studies that offer integrated solutions to security and privacy problems.

Hardcover ISBN: 978-1-53612-942-7
Retail Price: $195

Cyber-Security and Information Warfare

Editor: Nicholas J. Daras

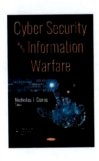

Series: Cybercrime and Cybersecurity Research

Book Description: A variety of modern research methods in a number of innovating cyber-security techniques and information management technologies are provided in this book along with new related mathematical developments and support applications from engineering.

Hardcover ISBN: 978-1-53614-385-0
Retail Price: $230

To see a complete list of Nova publications, please visit our website at www.novapublishers.com